PHILIP'S ESSENTIAL SCHOOL ATLAS

Published in Great Britain in 2019 by Philip's,
a division of Octopus Publishing Group Limited
(www.octopusbooks.co.uk)
Carmelite House, 50 Victoria Embankment
London EC4Y 0DZ
An Hachette UK Company
(www.hachette.co.uk)

Printed in Malaysia

Cartography by Philip's
Previously published as
Philip's Student Atlas

Copyright © 2019 Philip's

Hardback Edition
ISBN 978-1-84907-518-3
Paperback Edition
ISBN 978-1-84907-519-0

Details of other Philip's titles and services can be found on our website at:
www.philips-maps.co.uk

MAP SYMBOLS

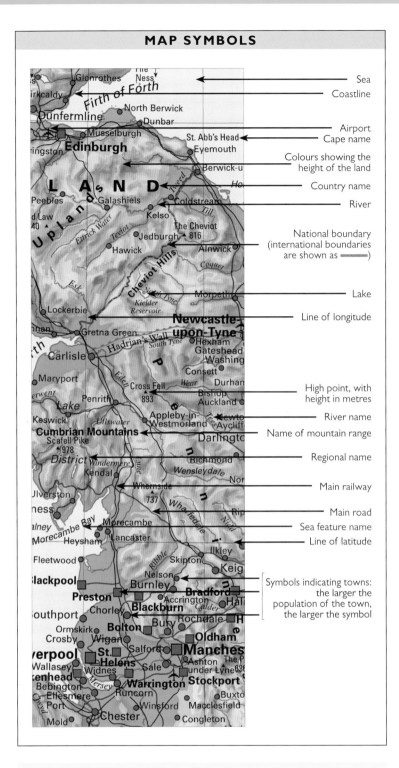

Sea
Coastline
Airport
Cape name
Colours showing the height of the land
Country name
River
National boundary (international boundaries are shown as ▬▬▬)
Lake
Line of longitude
High point, with height in metres
River name
Name of mountain range
Regional name
Main railway
Main road
Sea feature name
Line of latitude
Symbols indicating towns: the larger the population of the town, the larger the symbol

HEIGHT OF LAND

There is an explanation like this one on every page where different colours are used to show the height of the land above sea level.

The highest point in a region is shown with the symbol ▲ plus the height in metres.

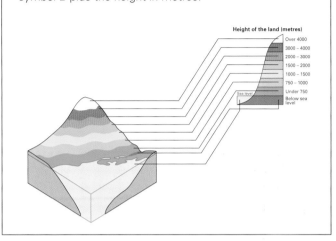

Height of the land (metres)

Over 4000
3000 – 4000
2000 – 3000
1500 – 2000
1000 – 1500
750 – 1000
Under 750
Sea level
Below sea level

SCALE BAR

Every map has a scale statement, scale bar and ruler accompanying it. For a full explanation of scale and how to use the scale bar, see page 2.

Scale 1:48 000 000   1 cm on the map = 480 km on the ground

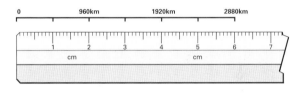

0   960km   1920km   2880km

SCALE COMPARISON MAP

This map, or one of the U.K. and Ireland, appears on most of the maps of the continents at the same scale as the main map. They give an idea of the size of that continent.

ENGLAND & WALES
on same scale

LOCATOR MAP

There is a small map such as this on every map page. The bright green area shows how the main map fits into its larger region.

Royal Geographical Society
with IBG

Advancing geography and geographical learning

Philip's World Atlases are published in association with The Royal Geographical Society (with The Institute of British Geographers).

The Society was founded in 1830 and given a Royal Charter in 1859 for 'the advancement of geographical science'. Today it is a leading world centre for geographical learning – supporting education, teaching, research and expeditions, and promoting public understanding of the subject.

Further information about the Society and how to join may be found on its website at: **www.rgs.org**

PHOTOGRAPHIC ACKNOWLEDGEMENTS
Alamy /Roger Bamber p. 24 (centre), / Ian Dagnall p.26, /Robert Evans p.24 (top), /Kevin Schafer p.61, /Stocktrek Images, Inc. p. 36; **Corbis** /Tim Graham p. 24 (bottom), /Reuters p. 44, /Royalty Free p. 73; **Crown Copyright** p. 7 (map extract); **Fotolia.co.uk** p. 76; **NPA Satellite Mapping, CGG Services (UK) Ltd** pp. 8, 9, 10, 12, 26, 27, 37, 49, 60, 74, 78, 79; **Patricia and Angus Macdonald** p. 7; **NASA** p. 11; **Precision Terrain Surveys Ltd** p. 6; **Front cover** Horvath Zoltan/Dreamstime.com.

Map data

Page 6: The Edinburgh city plan is based on mapping data licensed from Ordnance Survey® with the permission of the Controller of Her Majesty's Stationery Office. © Crown copyright 2018. All rights reserved. Licence number 100011710.

Scale and Direction

TYPES OF SCALE

In this atlas the scale of the map is shown in three ways:

WRITTEN STATEMENT

This tells you how many kilometres on the Earth are represented by one centimetre on the map.

1 cm on the map = 20 km on the ground

SCALE RATIO

This tells you that one unit on the map represents two million of the same unit on the ground.

Scale 1:2 000 000

SCALE BAR

This shows you the scale as a line or bar with a section of ruler beneath it.

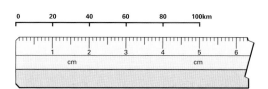

HOW TO MEASURE DISTANCE

The map on the right is a small part of the map of Southern Europe, which is on page 34 in the World section of the atlas.

The scale of the map extract is shown below:

Scale 1:10 000 000 1 cm on the map = 100 km on the ground

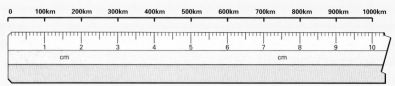

To measure the distance from London to Paris you can use any of the three methods described above.

For example:

USING THE WRITTEN STATEMENT

Using the scale above, you can see that 1 centimetre on the map represents 100 kilometres on the ground.

Measure the distance on the map between London and Paris. You will see that this is about 3.5 centimetres.

If 1 cm = 100 km

then 3.5 cm = 350 km (3.5 x 100)

USING THE SCALE RATIO

Using the scale above, you can see that the ratio is 1:10 000 000.

We know that the distance on the map between the cities is 3.5 cm and we know from the ratio that 1 cm on the map = 10 000 000 cm on the ground.

We multiply the map distance by the ratio.

= 3.5 x 10 000 000 cm
= 35 000 000 cm
= 350 000 m
= 350 km

USING THE SCALE BAR

We know that the distance on the map between the cities is 3.5 centimetres.

Measure 3.5 cm along the scale bar (or use the ruler as a guide) and read off the distance in kilometres.

Using these three methods, now work out the distance between London and Cardiff on the map above.

The map on the left is an extract from the map of Asia on page 39 in the World section of the atlas. Below, you can see the scale of this map. See if you can calculate the distance between Kolkata and Bangkok.

Scale 1:48 000 000 1 cm on the map = 480 km on the ground

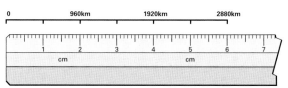

DIFFERENT SIZES OF SCALE

The table on the right shows the distances from London to Paris and Bangkok to Kolkata on the maps on page 2. The map distances are both 3.5 centimetres, but the distances on the ground are very different. This is because the maps are at different scales.

Included on most of the continent maps, in the World section of this atlas, are **scale comparison maps**. These show you the size of the UK and Ireland, or England and Wales, drawn at the same scale as the main map on that page. This is to give you an idea of the size of that continent.

	Map Distance	Map Scale	Distance on the Ground
London – Paris	3.5 centimetres	1:10 000 000	350 kilometres
Bangkok – Kolkata	3.5 centimetres	1:48 000 000	1,680 kilometres

Below are three maps which appear in this atlas:

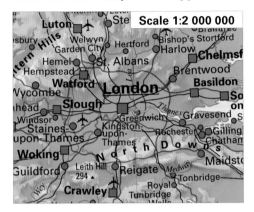

Scale 1:2 000 000

Scale 1:7 500 000

Scale 1:20 000 000

These maps all show London, but the map above shows much more detail than the maps on the right. The map above is a larger-scale map than the maps on the right.

A **large-scale** map shows more detail of a **small** area.

A **small-scale** map shows less detail of a **large** area.

Notice how the scale ratios at the top right of each map are getting larger as the scale of the map gets smaller.

DIRECTION ON THE MAPS

On most of the atlas maps, north is at the top of the page. Lines of latitude cross the maps from east to west. Longitude lines run from south to north. These usually curve a little because the Earth is a globe and not a flat shape.

POINTS OF THE COMPASS

Below is a drawing of the points of a compass. North, east, south and west are called **cardinal points**. Direction is sometimes given in degrees. This is measured clockwise from north. To help you remember the order of the compass points, try to learn this sentence:

Naughty **E**lephants **S**quirt **W**ater

USING A COMPASS

Compasses have a needle with a magnetic tip. The tip is attracted towards the Magnetic North Pole, which is close to the Geographical North Pole. The compass tells you where north is. You can see the Magnetic North Pole on the diagram below.

ACTIVITIES

Look at the map below.
If Ambleside is east of Belfast then:

• Valencia is _____ of Belfast;

• Renfrew is _____ of Ambleside;

• Oxford is _____ of Plymouth;

• Belfast is _____ of Oxford;

• Plymouth is _____ of Renfrew.

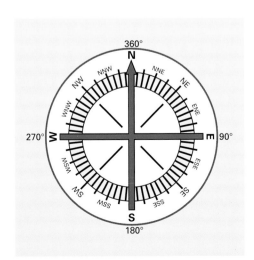

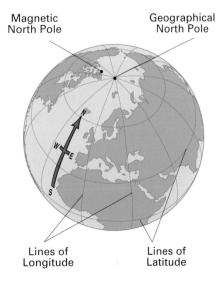

Magnetic North Pole   Geographical North Pole

Lines of Longitude   Lines of Latitude

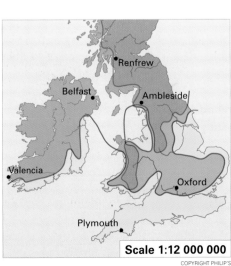

Scale 1:12 000 000

COPYRIGHT PHILIP'S

LATITUDE

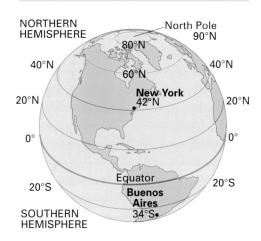

LONGITUDE

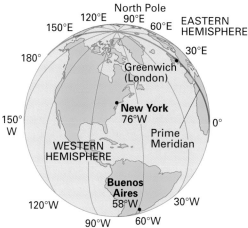

USING LATITUDE & LONGITUDE

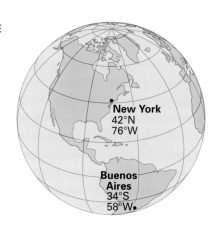

Lines of latitude cross the atlas maps from east to west. The **Equator** is at 0°. All other lines of latitude are either north of the Equator, or south of the Equator. Line 40°N is almost halfway towards the North Pole. The North Pole is at 90°N. At the Equator, a degree of longitude measures about 110 km.

Lines of longitude run from north to south. These lines meet at the North Pole and the South Pole. Longitude 0° passes through Greenwich. This line is also called the Prime Meridian. Lines of longitude are either east of 0° or west of 0°. There are 180 degrees of longitude both east and west of 0°.

There are 60 minutes in a degree. Latitude and longitude lines make a grid. You can find a place if you know its latitude and longitude number. The latitude number is either north or south of the Equator. The longitude number is either east or west of the Greenwich Meridian.

SPECIAL LATITUDE LINES

The Earth's axis is tilted at an angle of approximately 23½°. In June, the northern hemisphere is tilted towards the Sun. On 21 June the Sun is directly overhead at the **Tropic of Cancer**, 23°26'N, and this is midsummer in the northern hemisphere. Midsummer in the southern hemisphere occurs on 21 December, when the Sun is overhead at the **Tropic of Capricorn**, 23°26'S. On the maps in this atlas these are shown as blue dotted lines.

In the North and South Polar regions there are places where the Sun does not rise or set above the horizon at certain times of the year. These places are also shown by a blue dotted line on the maps. The **Arctic Circle** is at 66°34'N and the **Antarctic Circle** is at 66°34'S.

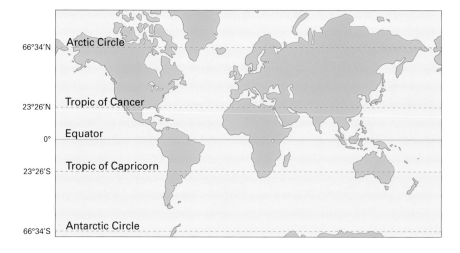

LATITUDE AND LONGITUDE IN THIS ATLAS

In this atlas lines of latitude and longitude are coloured blue.

On large-scale maps, such as those of England and Wales on pages 16–17, there is a line for every degree. On smaller-scale maps only every other, every fifth or even tenth line is shown.

The map on the right shows the UK and Ireland. The latitude and longitude lines are numbered at the edges of the map. The bottom of the map shows whether a place is east or west of Greenwich. The side of the map tells you how far north from the Equator the line is.

Around the edges of the map are small yellow pointers with letters or figures in their boxes. Columns made by longitude lines have letters in their boxes; rows made by latitude lines have figures.

In the index at the end of the atlas, places have figure-letter references as well as latitude and longitude numbers to help you locate the place names on the maps.

On the map opposite, London is in rectangle **8M** (this is where row 8 crosses with column M). Edinburgh is in **4J** and Dublin is in **6F**.

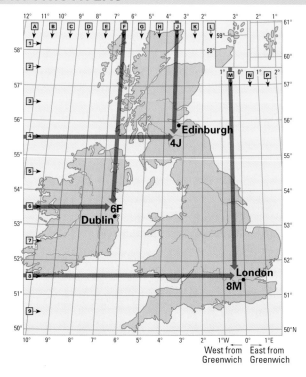

HOW TO FIND A PLACE

The map on the right is an extract from the map of Scotland on page 18. If you want to find Stornoway in the atlas, you must look in the index. Places are listed alphabetically. You will find the following entry:

Stornoway .... 58° 13'N 6° 23'W **18 1B**

The first number in **bold** type is the page number where the map appears. The figure and letter which follow the page number give the grid rectangle on the map in which the feature appears. Here we can see that Stornoway is on page 18 in the rectangle where row 1 crosses column B.

The latitude and longitude number corresponds with the numbered lines on the map. The first set of figures represent the latitude and the second set represent the longitude. The unit of measurement for latitude and longitude is the degree (°) which is divided into minutes (').

Latitude and longitude can be used to locate places more accurately on smaller-scale maps such as those in the World section. A more detailed explanation of how to estimate the minutes can be found on page 90.

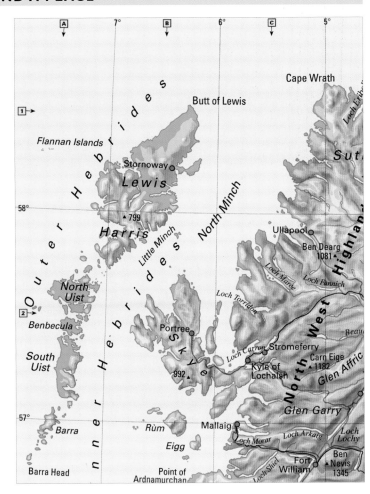

MAKING MAPS

One of the greatest problems in making maps is how to draw the curved surface of the globe on a flat piece of paper. As a globe is three dimensional, it is not possible to show its surface on a flat map without some form of distortion.

This map (right) shows one way of putting the globe on to paper, but because it splits up the land and sea it is not very useful.

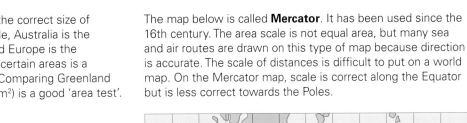

The map below is better because it shows the correct size of places. It is an **equal-area map**. For example, Australia is the correct size in relation to North America, and Europe is the correct size in relation to Africa. Comparing certain areas is a useful way to check the accuracy of maps. Comparing Greenland (2.2 million km²) with Australia (7.7 million km²) is a good 'area test'.

The map below is called **Mercator**. It has been used since the 16th century. The area scale is not equal area, but many sea and air routes are drawn on this type of map because direction is accurate. The scale of distances is difficult to put on a world map. On the Mercator map, scale is correct along the Equator but is less correct towards the Poles.

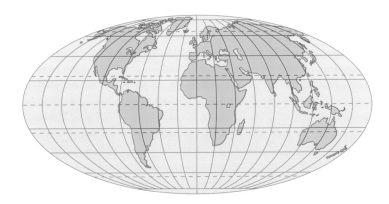

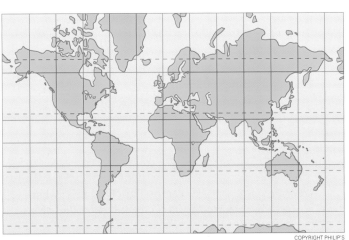

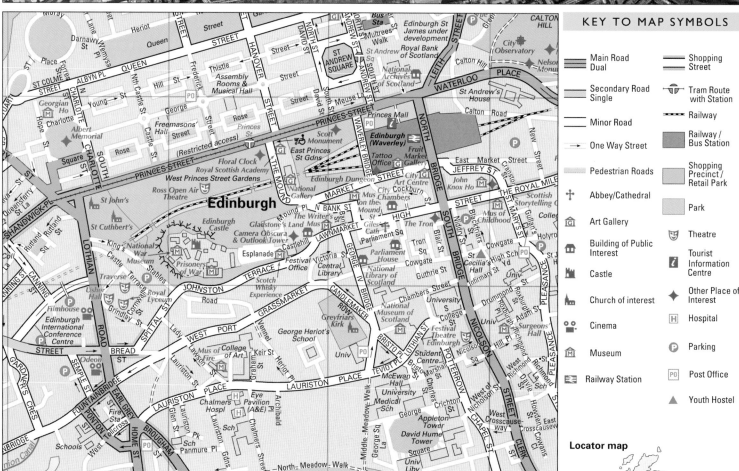

KEY TO MAP SYMBOLS

Main Road Dual	Shopping Street
Secondary Road Single	Tram Route with Station
Minor Road	Railway
One Way Street	Railway / Bus Station
Pedestrian Roads	Shopping Precinct / Retail Park
✝ Abbey/Cathedral	Park
Art Gallery	Theatre
Building of Public Interest	Tourist Information Centre
Castle	Other Place of Interest
Church of interest	H Hospital
Cinema	P Parking
Museum	PO Post Office
Railway Station	▲ Youth Hostel

Scale 1:10 000 1 centimetre on the map and aerial photograph = 100 metres on the ground

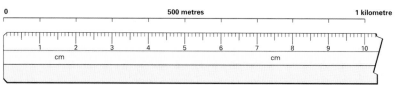

Locator map

KEY TO MAP SYMBOLS

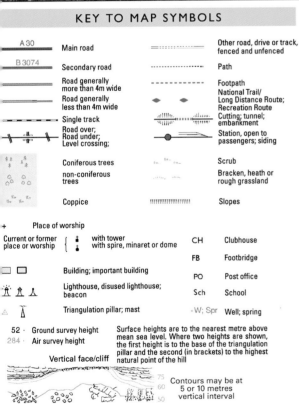

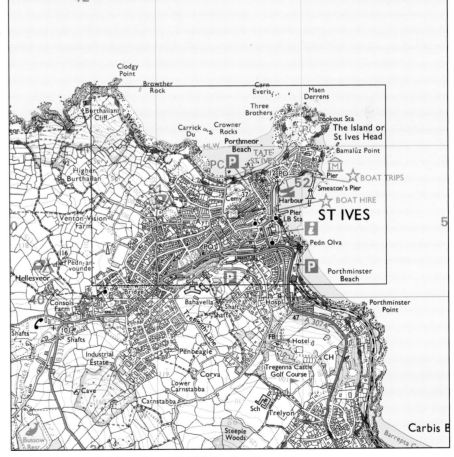

Reproduced from the 2008 Ordnance Survey 1:25,000 Explorer Map with permission of the controller of Her Majesty's Stationery office © Crown Copyright

Scale of photograph 1:10 000

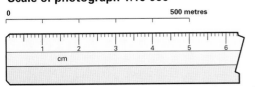

1 centimetre on the photograph = 100 metres on the ground

Scale of map 1:25 000

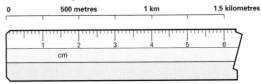

1 centimetre on the map = 250 metres on the ground

Map Reading from Satellite Imagery

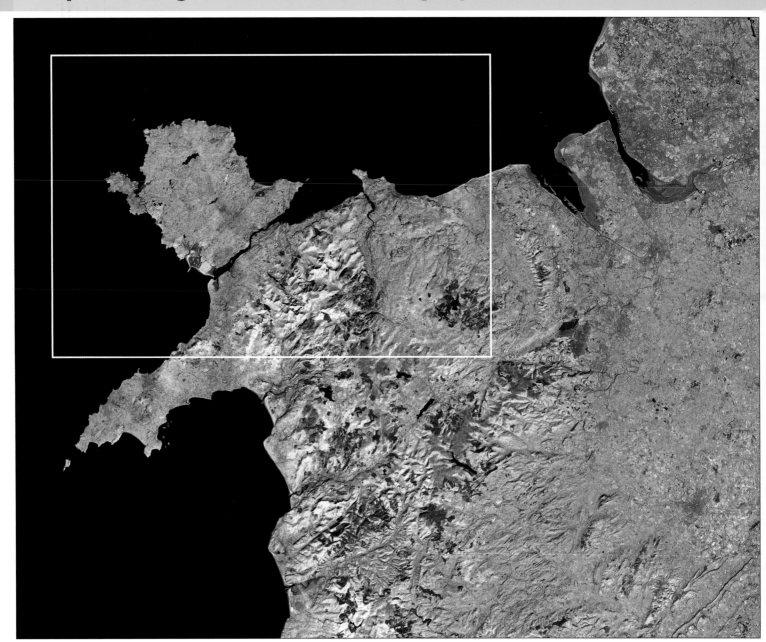

KEY TO MAP SYMBOLS

◉◉◉◎◉◎ ○ ○ ○   Town symbols

(built-up area symbol)	Built-up areas	————	Main passenger railways
CONWY	Administrative area names	————	Other passenger railways
SNOWDONIA	National park names	✈	Major airports
═══════	Motorways	～～	Rivers
————	Major roads	(lake symbol)	Lakes or reservoirs
————	Other important roads	▲ 1085	Elevation in metres
- - - -	Administrative boundaries	■	Place of interest

Locator map

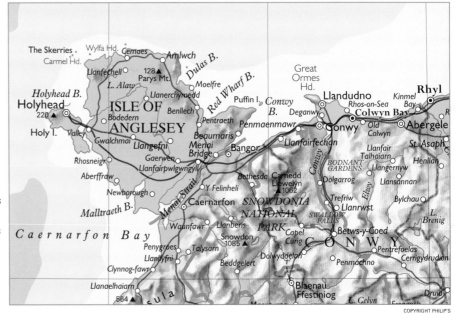

COPYRIGHT PHILIP'S

Scale 1:760 000   1 cm on the map and satellite image = 7.6km on the ground

0	38km	76km

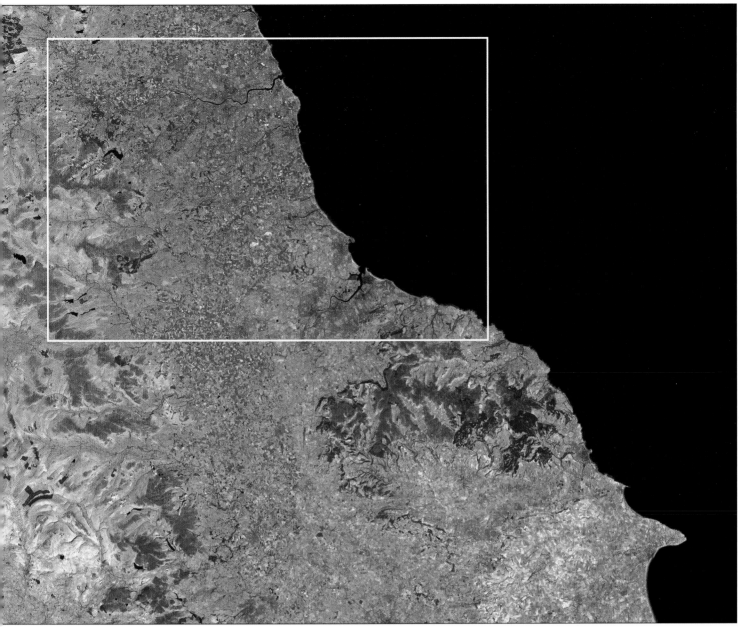

SATELLITE IMAGERY

[Th]e images on these pages were produced by the
[La]ndsat 7 satellite, launched by NASA in 1999.
[It] travels around the Earth at a height of over
[70]0 km. It is able to scan every part of the Earth's
[su]rface once every 16 days. The data is
[tra]nsmitted back to Earth where it is printed in
[fa]lse colours to make certain features stand out.
[   ]On these pages grass and crops appear light
[gr]een, soils and exposed rock light grey, woodland
[da]rk green, moorland brown, water black and
[bu]ilt-up areas dark grey. The image on this page
[sh]ows North-east England and the image on page
[ ]shows North Wales. Both images were
[re]corded in late March. Comparing the maps,
[wh]ich are taken from *Philip's Modern School Atlas*,
[wi]th the images helps identify specific features on
[th]e images.

Locator map

COPYRIGHT PHILIP'S

Scale 1:760 000   1 cm on the map and satellite image = 7.6km on the ground

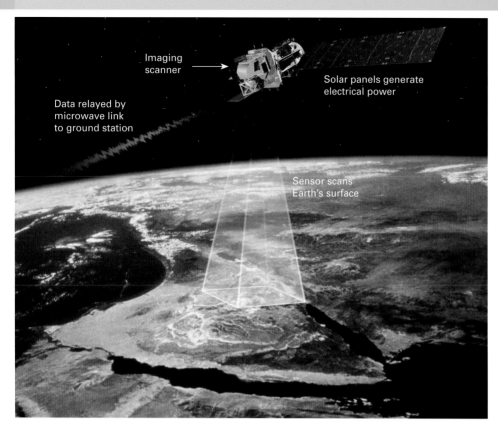

◄ Earth Observation Satellites

Powered by outstretched solar panels, Earth Observation Satellites, such as the one shown here, can collect and relay back to Earth huge volumes of geographical data which is then processed and stored on computers.

Depending on the sensors fitted, the choice of orbit and altitude, these satellites can provide detailed imagery of the Earth's surface at close range or monitor environmental issues covering the entire world. Objects less than 1 metre across can now be seen from space as well as the entire surface of our planet, allowing us to monitor issues such as the atmosphere, land and sea temperature, vegetation, rainfall and ice cover.

The importance of recording this information over time is that it enables us to see long-term changes and increases our understanding of the processes involved. Some satellites have been collecting data for over 25 years. A few of their uses are shown on this page and the page opposite.

▲ The River Thames, London

This image shows central London from St Paul's Cathedral, in the upper left-hand corner, across to the Tower of London and Tower Bridge on the right-hand side. The image was captured from a satellite 680 km above the Earth and travelling at 6 km per second. It was captured at about midday in late October, the low sun showing clearly the shadows of the Shard and the chimney of Tate Modern. *(Image © EUSI, Inc. All Rights Reserved/NPA Satellite Mapping)*

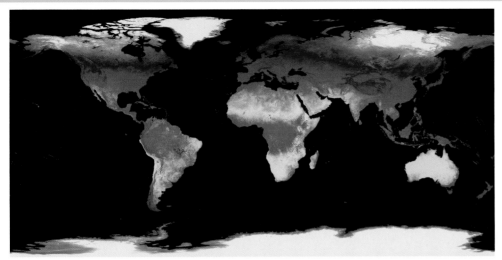

◄ World Land Surface Temperature, November
The satellite which captured this data uses another set of sensors that enable it to capture different data and over a much wider area. The colours range from light blue, indicating –25°C, through reds and oranges up to yellow, indicating +45°C. The land surface temperature thus shows the beginning of winter north of the Equator and summer south of the Equator.

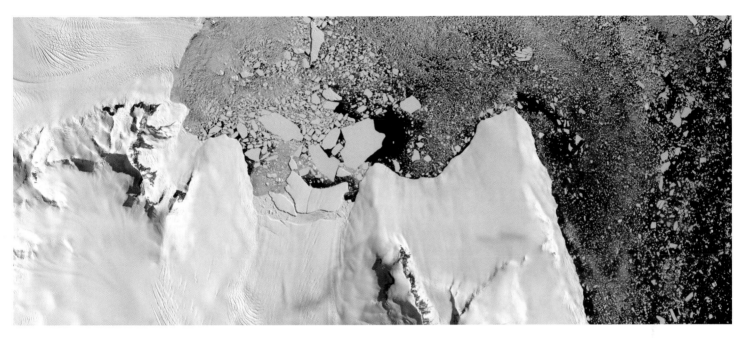

▲ Ice Cover, Alexander Island, Antarctica
An important use for satellites is to monitor inaccessible areas of the world that are environmentally sensitive, such as the ice caps surrounding the North and South Poles. This image shows the Hampton Glacier, which is at the foot of the image, flowing towards the sea. The ice then breaks off into a series of icebergs, which can be seen at the top. Because satellites revisit these areas regularly, changes to the extent of the ice can be monitored.

▲ Weather
Weather satellites travel at the same speed as the Earth's rotation and stay in daylight to allow them to monitor the same area for major storms and other events. In order to capture as much of the Earth's surface as possible, they orbit farther out in space, about 35,000 km above the Earth's surface. This image clearly shows a hurricane approaching the coast of central America and the Gulf of Mexico.

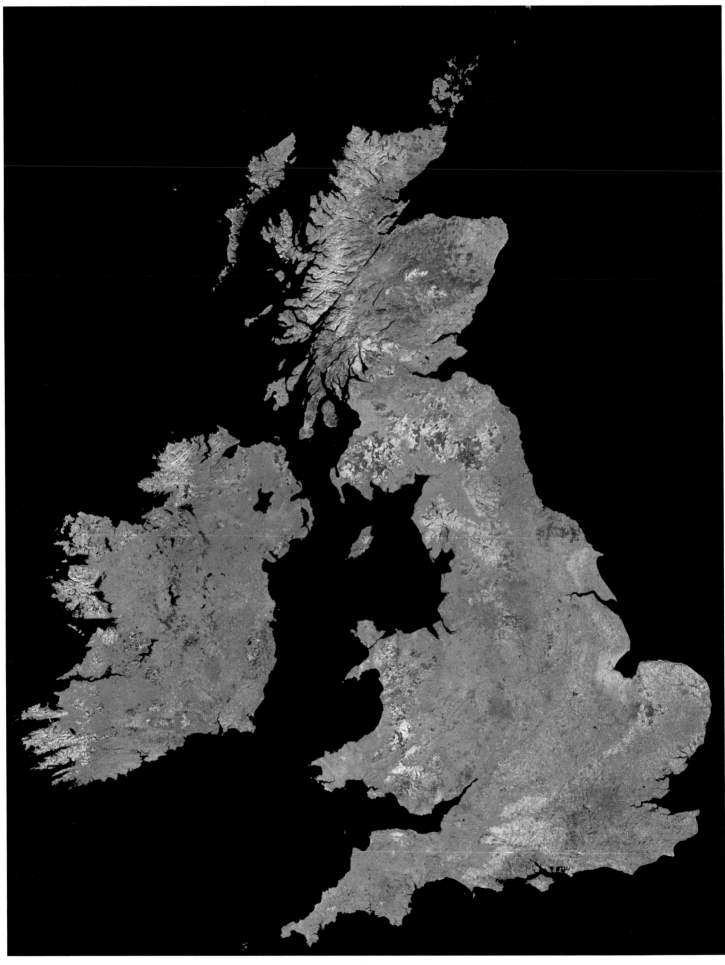

▲ The United Kingdom and Ireland, seen from Space

The colours on this image have been processed to match the natural tone of the landscape. The large amount of agricultural land in the UK is reflected by the extensive green on the image. In Scotland, the snow-covered Cairngorm Mountains can be seen, with brownish-green coniferous forests below the snow line. Most of Ireland has a mid-green colour, which indicates the presence of rich pasture. In the west, the lighter colour indicates moorland or bare rock and is also visible in the Cambrian Mountains in Wales, the Pennines and the Lake District in England, and the Scottish Highlands. Urban areas are shown as dark grey in colour.

Scale 1:4 600 000   1 cm on the map = 46 km on the ground

0   100km   200km   300km   400km

Height of the land (metres)

over 1000
400–1000
200–400
100–200
0–100
sea level
below sea level

	Highest mountains
	Largest lakes
	Longest rivers

England
Scafell Pike — 978m
Windermere — 15km²
Thames — 346km
Severn — 354km

Wales
Snowdon — 1085m
Bala Lake — 5km²
Tywi — 109km
Severn — 354km

Scotland
Ben Nevis — 1345m
Loch Lomond — 70km²
Tay — 188km

Northern Ireland
Slieve Donard — 852m
Lough Neagh — 396km²
Bann — 128.7km

Ireland
Carrauntoohill — 1041m
Lough Corrib — 176km²
Shannon — 370km

ATLANTIC

OCEAN

Shetland Islands
Unst
Yell
Mainland
Foula
Fair Isle

Orkney Islands
Westray
Sanday
Mainland
Hoy
Pentland Firth
Duncansby Head

North Rona

Lewis
Harris
799
St. Kilda
North Uist
Benbecula
South Uist
Barra

Outer Hebrides
Inner Hebrides

Skye
1182
Rùm
Eigg
Coll
Tiree
Mull
Colonsay

North West Highlands
Cape Wrath
Dornoch Firth
Moray Firth
Kinnairds Head
Spey
Loch Ness
Ben Macdhui 1309
Grampian Mountains
Don
Dee
Ben Nevis 1345
1214
Tay

Loch Lomond
Firth of Forth
Jura
Islay
Clyde
Southern Uplands
St. Abb's Head
Holy Island
The Cheviot 816
843
840
Tweed

Arran
Firth of Clyde
North Channel
Mull of Galloway
Solway Firth
Tyne

Malin Head
Rathlin Island
Arranmore
752
Mourne
Bann 554
683
Donegal Bay
Lower Lough Erne
644
Lough Neagh
852 Slieve Donard
620
Isle of Man

Erris Head
Achill Island
819
Lough Mask
Lough Corrib
Lough Ree
Boyne
Liffey
Galway Bay
Aran Islands
Shannon
Lough Derg
920
Barrow
Suir
Blackwater
953
1041
Dingle Bay
Carrauntoohill
Lee
Bantry Bay
Fastnet Rock
Cape Clear

Ireland

Irish Sea

Wicklow Mountains 926

Lake District
Scafell Pike 978
Windermere
Morecambe Bay

Liverpool Bay
Anglesey
Mersey
The Peak 636

Pennines
893
Tees
North York Moors 454

Great Britain

North Sea

Flamborough Head
Spurn Head
Humber
The Wash
The Fens
Great Ouse
Yare
Lowestoft Ness

Aire
Ouse
Trent
Nene

Snowdon 1085
Bala Lake
Cambrian Mountains
Dee
Severn
Wye
Avon
315
330
Cotswold Hills
Chiltern Hills
Thames

Cardigan Bay
St. David's Head
Tywi
Brecon Beacons 886
St. George's Channel
Carmarthen Bay

Salisbury Plain 297
North Downs
North Foreland
South Downs
Beachy Head
Strait of Dover

Bristol Channel
Lundy
Exmoor
Hartland Point
621 Dartmoor
Lyme Bay
Portland Bill
Isle of Wight

Celtic
Sea

Land's End
Isles of Scilly
Lizard
Start Point
Tamar

English Channel

Channel Islands
Guernsey
Jersey

France

West from Greenwich 0° East from Greenwich

COPYRIGHT PHILIP'S

COPYRIGHT PHILIP'S

COUNTRY FACTS

Country Name	Area (square kilometres)	Inhabitants (thousands 2015)	Capital City or Town
UNITED KINGDOM	**240,883**	**66,040**	**LONDON**
of which England	129,652	55,619	London
Wales	20,628	3,125	Cardiff
Scotland	77,097	5,425	Edinburgh
Northern Ireland	13,532	1,871	Belfast
*Isle of Man	572	84	Douglas
* Jersey	116	100	St. Helier
*Guernsey	63	63	St. Peter Port
IRELAND	**68,896**	**5,068**	**DUBLIN**

* Crown Dependencies which are not part of the U.K.

Scale 1:4 600 000

SCOTLAND
1. ABERDEEN CITY
2. DUNDEE CITY
3. WEST DUNBARTONSHIRE
4. EAST DUNBARTONSHIRE
5. CITY OF GLASGOW
6. INVERCLYDE
7. RENFREWSHIRE
8. EAST RENFREWSHIRE
9. NORTH LANARKSHIRE
10. FALKIRK
11. CLACKMANNANSHIRE
12. WEST LOTHIAN
13. CITY OF EDINBURGH
14. MIDLOTHIAN

WALES
15. SWANSEA
16. NEATH PORT TALBOT
17. BRIDGEND
18. RHONDDA CYNON TAFF
19. MERTHYR TYDFIL
20. CAERPHILLY
21. BLAENAU GWENT
22. TORFAEN
23. CARDIFF
24. NEWPORT

ENGLAND
25. HARTLEPOOL
26. DARLINGTON
27. STOCKTON-ON-TEES
28. MIDDLESBROUGH
29. REDCAR AND CLEVELAND
30. BLACKPOOL
31. BLACKBURN WITH DARWEN
32. HALTON
33. WARRINGTON
34. KINGSTON UPON HULL
35. NORTH EAST LINCOLNSHIRE
36. STOKE-ON-TRENT
37. TELFORD AND WREKIN
38. DERBY CITY
39. CITY OF NOTTINGHAM
40. LEICESTER CITY
41. RUTLAND
42. PETERBOROUGH
43. MILTON KEYNES
44. LUTON
45. NORTH SOMERSET
46. CITY OF BRISTOL
47. BATH AND N. E. SOMERSET
48. SWINDON
49. READING
50. WOKINGHAM
51. WINDSOR AND MAIDENHEAD
52. SLOUGH
53. BRACKNELL FOREST
54. THURROCK
55. SOUTHEND-ON-SEA
56. MEDWAY
57. PLYMOUTH
58. TORBAY
59. POOLE
60. BOURNEMOUTH
61. SOUTHAMPTON
62. PORTSMOUTH
63. BRIGHTON AND HOVE
64. BEDFORD
65. CENTRAL BEDFORDSHIRE

The map shows the 11 districts in Northern Ireland, the 32 unitary authorities in Wales and the 55 unitary authorities in England. Authorities which are too small to name on the map are numbered and listed separately.

Greater London and the 6 English metropolitan counties are coloured white on the map.

Greater London is divided into 32 borough councils and the City of London.

The 6 English metropolitan counties have 36 district councils.

● Capital cities

COPYRIGHT PHILIP'S

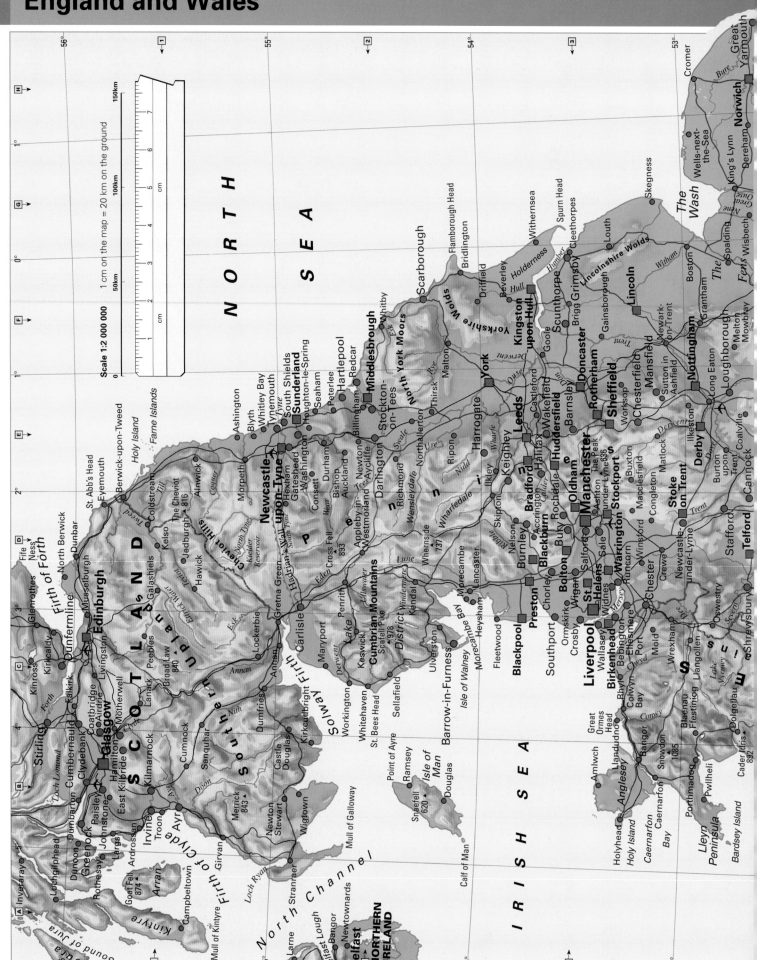

Scale 1:2 000 000

1 cm on the map = 20 km on the ground

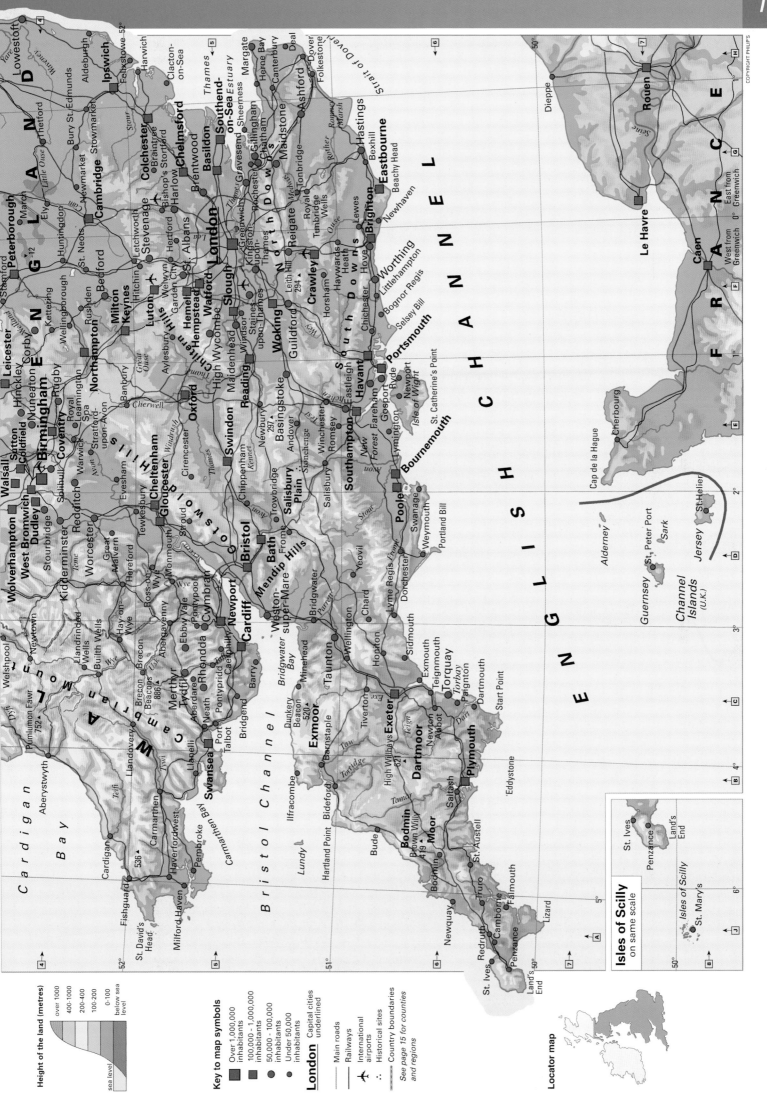

Height of the land (metres)
over 1000
400-1000
200-400
100-200
0-100
sea level
below sea level

Key to map symbols

■ Over 1,000,000 inhabitants
■ 100,000 - 1,000,000 inhabitants
● 50,000 - 100,000 inhabitants
• Under 50,000 inhabitants

London Capital cities underlined

—— Main roads
—— Railways
✈ International airports
∴ Historical sites
—— Country boundaries
See page 15 for counties and regions

Isles of Scilly
on same scale

St. Ives
Penzance
Land's End
Isles of Scilly
St. Mary's

Locator map

COPYRIGHT PHILIP'S

Orkney Islands
on same scale

Shetland Islands
on same scale

Locator map

Scale 1:2 000 000   1 cm on the map = 20 km on the ground

0   50km   100km   150km   200km

COPYRIGHT PHILIP'S

Height of the land (metres)

| over 1000 |
| 400-1000 |
| 200-400 |
| 100-200 |
| 0-100 |
| below sea level |

sea level

Key to map symbols

- Over 1,000,000 inhabitants
- 100,000 – 1,000,000 inhabitants
- 50,000 – 100,000 inhabitants
- Under 50,000 inhabitants

Dublin Capital cities underlined

Scale 1:2 000 000

— Main roads
— Railways
✈ International airports
‑‑‑ Country boundaries

See page 15 for counties and regions

COPYRIGHT PHILIP'S

Locator map

Weather is measured in terms of rainfall, temperature, cloudiness, sunshine and wind over a short period of time, usually less than a day. Climate is the average of the weather over a longer period, usually 30 years.

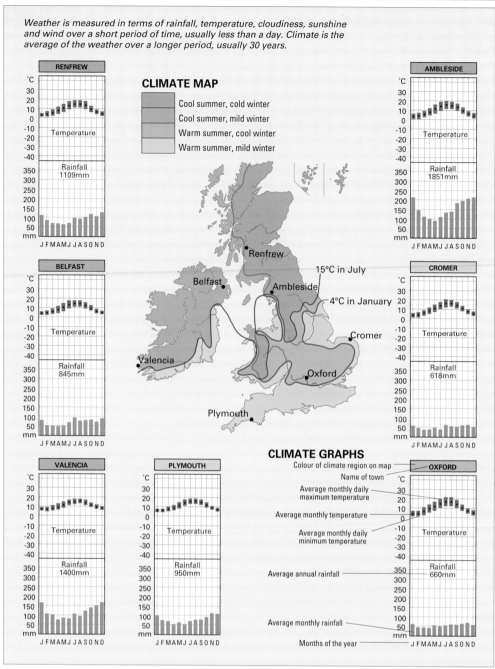

CLIMATE MAP

CLIMATE MAP legend:
- Cool summer, cold winter
- Cool summer, mild winter
- Warm summer, cool winter
- Warm summer, mild winter

RENFREW — Temperature, Rainfall 1109mm
AMBLESIDE — Temperature, Rainfall 1851mm
BELFAST — Temperature, Rainfall 845mm
CROMER — Temperature, Rainfall 618mm
VALENCIA — Temperature, Rainfall 1400mm
PLYMOUTH — Temperature, Rainfall 950mm
OXFORD — Temperature, Rainfall 660mm

Map labels: Renfrew, Belfast, Ambleside, 15°C in July, 4°C in January, Cromer, Valencia, Oxford, Plymouth

CLIMATE GRAPHS

- Colour of climate region on map
- Name of town
- Average monthly daily maximum temperature
- Average monthly temperature
- Average monthly daily minimum temperature
- Average annual rainfall
- Average monthly rainfall
- Months of the year

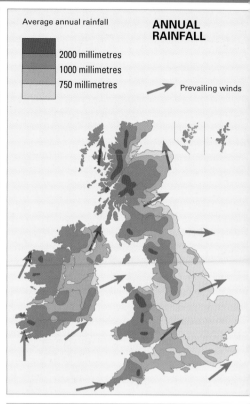

ANNUAL RAINFALL

Average annual rainfall
- 2000 millimetres
- 1000 millimetres
- 750 millimetres
- → Prevailing winds

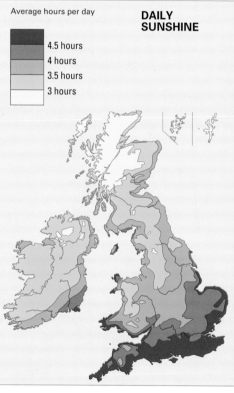

DAILY SUNSHINE

Average hours per day
- 4.5 hours
- 4 hours
- 3.5 hours
- 3 hours

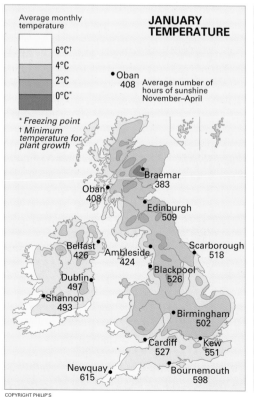

JANUARY TEMPERATURE

Average monthly temperature
- 6°C †
- 4°C
- 2°C
- 0°C *

* Freezing point
† Minimum temperature for plant growth

Oban 408 — Average number of hours of sunshine November–April

Braemar 383
Oban 408
Edinburgh 509
Belfast 426
Ambleside 424
Scarborough 518
Blackpool 526
Dublin 497
Shannon 493
Birmingham 502
Cardiff 527
Kew 551
Newquay 615
Bournemouth 598

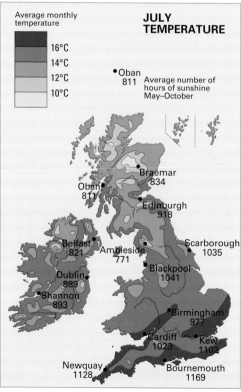

JULY TEMPERATURE

Average monthly temperature
- 16°C
- 14°C
- 12°C
- 10°C

Oban 811 — Average number of hours of sunshine May–October

Braemar 834
Oban 811
Edinburgh 918
Belfast 821
Ambleside 771
Scarborough 1035
Blackpool 1041
Dublin 889
Shannon 893
Birmingham 977
Cardiff 1023
Kew 1102
Newquay 1128
Bournemouth 1169

Temperature Records
Highest
38.5°C Brogdale near Faversham, (Kent) 10 August 2003
Lowest
-27.2°C Braemar, Aberdeenshire, 10 January 1982 and 11 February 1895, Altnaharra, Highland, 30 December 1995

Rainfall Records
Highest 24 hour total
279 mm Martinstown, near Dorchester, Dorset, 18 July 1955
The highest total for any 24 hour period is 316mm at Seathwaite, Cumbria on 19 November 2009.

Sunshine Records
Highest monthly total
390 hours Eastbourne and Hastings, Sussex, July 1911
Lowest monthly total
0 hours Westminster, Greater London, December 1890

Winds (highest gusts)
150 knots Cairngorm, 20 March 1986

GEOLOGY

MINING

Minerals are rocks that are used as resources. A selection of places where minerals are mined are shown on the map. There is a separate map for energy sources on page 23. Rocks such as limestone, granite and sandstone which are used in the building industry as well as sand and gravel are quarried widely.

Cleveland (potash)

Navan (lead and zinc)

Winsford (salt)

Southern limit of glaciation

St. Austell (china clay)

Rock type		Geological Era
	Sands and clays	TERTIARY (0–65 million years old)
	Chalk	SECONDARY (65–230 million years old)
	Clays, sands, sandstone	
	Limestone	
	Coal measures	PRIMARY (230–570 million years old)
	Limestone, millstone grit	
	Sandstone	
	Shales and slates	
	Gneiss, quartzite, schists	Various ages
	Basalt and granite	

FLOOD RISK IN ENGLAND AND WALES

■ Areas at greatest risk from flooding

WATER SUPPLY

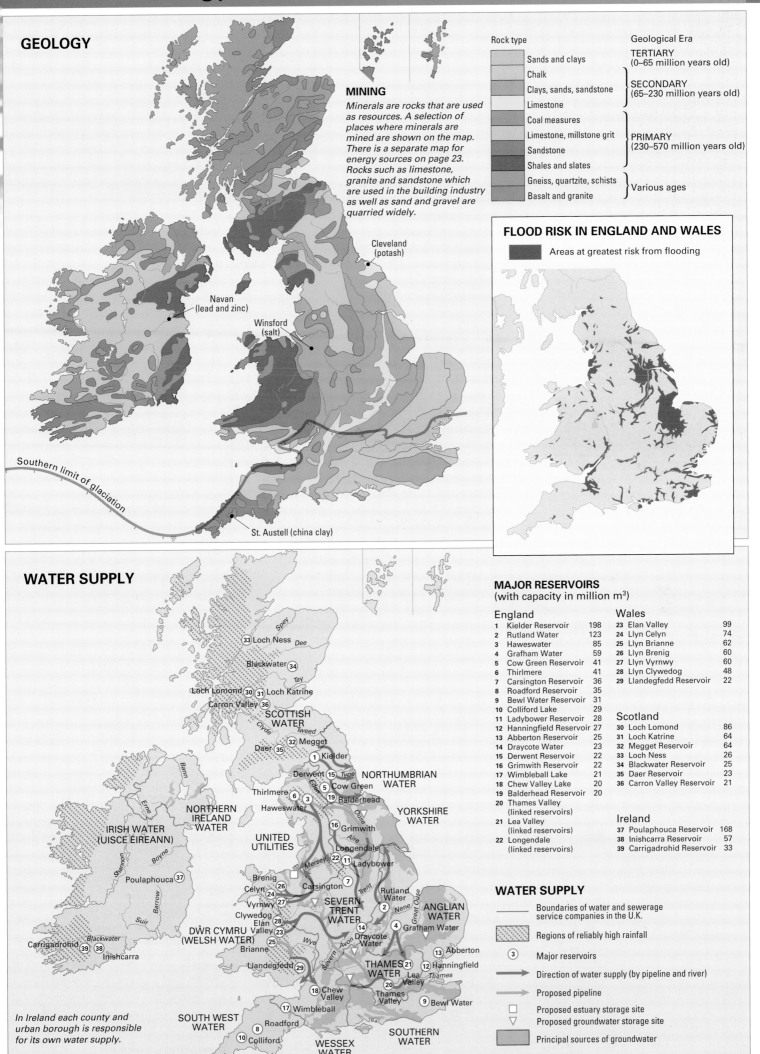

Spey
Loch Ness
Dee
Blackwater
Tay
Loch Lomond   Loch Katrine
Carron Valley
SCOTTISH WATER
Clyde   Tweed
Daer   Megget
Kielder
Derwent   Tyne   NORTHUMBRIAN WATER
Cow Green
Thirlmere   Eden
Haweswater   Balderhead   YORKSHIRE WATER
NORTHERN IRELAND WATER
Ouse
Grimwith
UNITED UTILITIES
Longendale
Mersey   Ladybower
Bann
IRISH WATER (UISCE ÉIREANN)
Erne
Brenig
Celyn
Carsington
Trent
Rutland Water
ANGLIAN WATER
Shannon
Boyne
Poulaphouca
Vyrnwy
SEVERN-TRENT WATER
Nene
Great Ouse
Grafham Water
Clywedog
Elan Valley
Barrow
DŴR CYMRU (WELSH WATER)
Abberton
Brianne
Wye
Draycote Water
Suir
Carrigadrohid   Blackwater
Inishcarra
Llandegfedd
Severn   Avon
THAMES WATER
Hanningfield
Lea Valley   Thames
Chew Valley
Thames Valley
Bewl Water
Wimbleball
SOUTH WEST WATER
Roadford
Colliford
WESSEX WATER
SOUTHERN WATER

In Ireland each county and urban borough is responsible for its own water supply.

MAJOR RESERVOIRS
(with capacity in million m³)

England

1	Kielder Reservoir	198
2	Rutland Water	123
3	Haweswater	85
4	Grafham Water	59
5	Cow Green Reservoir	41
6	Thirlmere	41
7	Carsington Reservoir	36
8	Roadford Reservoir	35
9	Bewl Water Reservoir	31
10	Colliford Lake	29
11	Ladybower Reservoir	28
12	Hanningfield Reservoir	27
13	Abberton Reservoir	25
14	Draycote Water	23
15	Derwent Reservoir	22
16	Grimwith Reservoir	22
17	Wimbleball Lake	21
18	Chew Valley Lake	20
19	Balderhead Reservoir	20
20	Thames Valley (linked reservoirs)	
21	Lea Valley (linked reservoirs)	
22	Longendale (linked reservoirs)	

Wales

23	Elan Valley	99
24	Llyn Celyn	74
25	Llyn Brianne	62
26	Llyn Brenig	60
27	Llyn Vyrnwy	60
28	Llyn Clywedog	48
29	Llandegfedd Reservoir	22

Scotland

30	Loch Lomond	86
31	Loch Katrine	64
32	Megget Reservoir	64
33	Loch Ness	26
34	Blackwater Reservoir	25
35	Daer Reservoir	23
36	Carron Valley Reservoir	21

Ireland

37	Poulaphouca Reservoir	168
38	Inishcarra Reservoir	57
39	Carrigadrohid Reservoir	33

WATER SUPPLY

— Boundaries of water and sewerage service companies in the U.K.

▨ Regions of reliably high rainfall

③ Major reservoirs

→ Direction of water supply (by pipeline and river)

→ Proposed pipeline

□ Proposed estuary storage site

▽ Proposed groundwater storage site

■ Principal sources of groundwater

COPYRIGHT PHILIP'S

TYPES OF FARM

- Dairy cattle
- Beef cattle
- Sheep
- Pigs and/or poultry
- Mixed farming
- Market gardening (fruit and vegetables)
- Cereals
- Other crops (mainly potatoes, sugar beet)
- Northern limit of 9 month growing season
- Forests
- Built-up areas

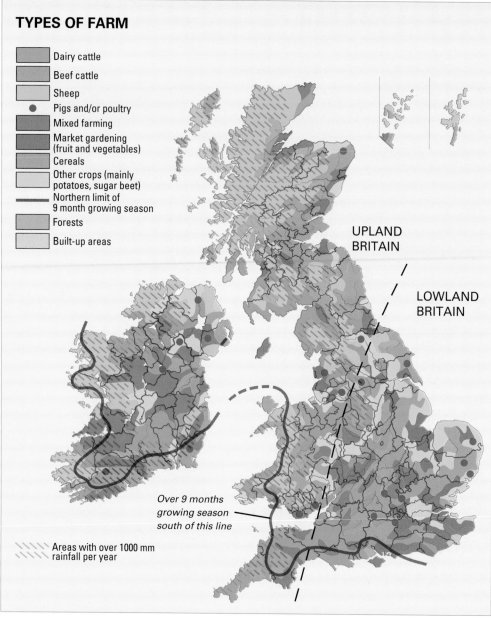

UPLAND BRITAIN

LOWLAND BRITAIN

Over 9 months growing season south of this line

Areas with over 1000 mm rainfall per year

CEREAL FARMING

The percentage of the total farmland used for growing cereals in 2016

- Over 40%
- 25 – 40%
- 10 – 25%
- 5 – 10%
- 0 – 5%

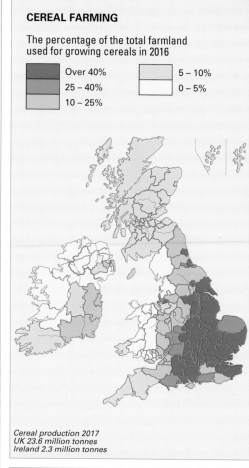

Cereal production 2017
UK 23.6 million tonnes
Ireland 2.3 million tonnes

DAIRY FARMING

The number of dairy cows per 100 hectares of farmland in 2016

- Over 40
- 30 – 40
- 20 – 30
- 10 – 20
- 0 – 10

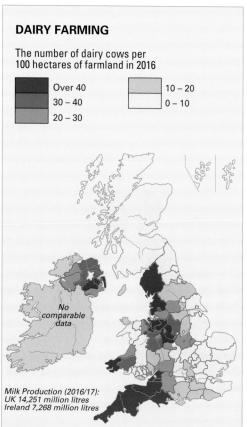

No comparable data

Milk Production (2016/17):
UK 14,251 million litres
Ireland 7,268 million litres

LIVESTOCK FARMING

The number of beef cattle, sheep and pigs per 100 hectares of farmland in 2017

- Over 400
- 300 – 400
- 200 – 300
- 100 – 200
- Under 100

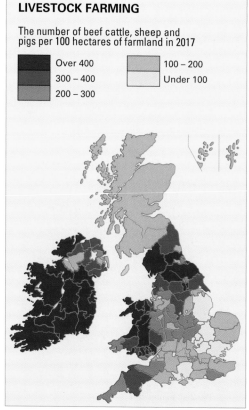

Scalloway — Lerwick
Scrabster
Kinlochbervie
West Coast of Scotland 191,701 tonnes
Ullapool
Fraserburgh
Peterhead
Mallaig
North Sea 321,568 tonnes
Killybegs
Kirkcudbright
Belfast
North Shields
Ardglass — Portavogie
Kilkeel — Douglas
Scarborough
Irish Sea 31,556 tonnes
Bridlington
Howth
Holyhead
Grimsby
Dingle
Dunmore East
Castletown
Bearhaven
Milford Haven
Leigh-on-Sea
Bristol Channel and Celtic Sea 11,750 tonnes
Shoreham
Brixham
Newlyn — Plymouth
English Channel 58,556 tonnes
West Ireland and Sole Bank 39,054 tonnes

FISHING

Major fishing ports by size of catch landed

- Mainly deep sea fish (e.g. cod)
- Mainly shallow sea fish (e.g. mackerel)
- Mainly shellfish e.g. lobster

The most important inshore fishing grounds

North Sea 321,568 tonnes
Total amount landed in each fishing region 2017

1000 500 200 100 50 m Depth of sea in metres

Faroe Islands

Norwegian Sea

NORWAY

ATLANTIC OCEAN

Magnus
Don
Tern
Statfjord
Harris
Brent
Gullfaks
Heather
Strathspey
Laggan
Ninian
Dunbar
Troll
Toremore
Clair
Cheviot
Oseberg
Sullom Voe
Nuggets
Bergen
Schiehallion
Rhum
Foinaven
Frigg
Shetland Islands
Kraken
Bruce
Boa
Haugesund
Beryl
Skene
Harding
Devenick
Orkney Islands
Crawford
East Brae
Flotta
Piper Brae
Sleipner
NORWEGIAN SECTOR
Captain
Thelma
Scott
Andrew
Beatrice
Britannia
Armada
Nigg
Forties
Everest
St. Fergus
Buzzard
Nelson
Peterhead
Durward
Lomond
Fasnakyle
Cruden Bay
Shearwater
Errochty
U.K. SECTOR
Rannoch
Clunie
Burgman
Fram
Joanne
Ekofisk
Cruachan
Lochay
Auk
DANISH SECTOR
Clachan
Sloy
Orion
Fife
Tyra
Longannet
Halfdan
Hunterston
Torness

NORTH SEA

Outer Hebrides

U.K. SECTOR

IRISH SECTOR

Ballylumford
Kilroot
Hartlepool
Breagh
Esmond
Cygnus
Teesside
Trent
DUTCH SECTOR
Millom
Salt End
Orca
Barrow in Furness
Ann
Carrack
K4B-K5A
Heysham
Drax
Morecambe
Ferrybridge
Viking
Lough Ree
Edenderry
Hamilton
Carrington
South Humber Bank
Point of Ayr
Eggborough
Leman
West Offaly
Poolbeg
Fiddler'sFerry
Dinorwig
Staythorpe
Moneypoint
Connahs Quay
West Burton
Turlough Hill
Ffestiniog
Cottam
Ardnacrusha
Ratcliffe-on-Soar
Bacton
Tarbert
Rugeley
Rheidol
Sizewell
Marina
Baglan Bay
Barking
Aghada
Grain
Kinsale Head
Aberthaw
Seabank
Irish Sea
Hinkley Point
Wytch Farm
Dungeness
Fawley
BELGIUM
Celtic Sea
English Channel
FRANCE

COPYRIGHT PHILIP'S

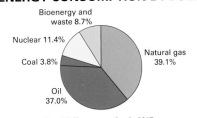

ENERGY CONSUMPTION BY FUEL

Bioenergy and waste 8.7%
Nuclear 11.4%
Coal 3.8%
Natural gas 39.1%
Oil 37.0%

Total U.K. consumption in 2017:
190.5 million tonnes of oil equivalent

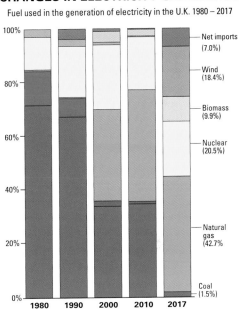

CHANGES IN ELECTRICITY GENERATION

Fuel used in the generation of electricity in the U.K. 1980 – 2017

100%
80%
60%
40%
20%
0%
1980 1990 2000 2010 2017

Net imports (7.0%)
Wind (18.4%)
Biomass (9.9%)
Nuclear (20.5%)
Natural gas (42.7%)
Coal (1.5%)

RENEWABLE ENERGY

The amount of energy generated from renewable sources in gigawatt hours, 2017

Over 25,000
20,000 - 25,000
10,000 - 20,000
5,000 - 10,000
Under 5,000

Major wind farm
Possible sites for tidal power generation

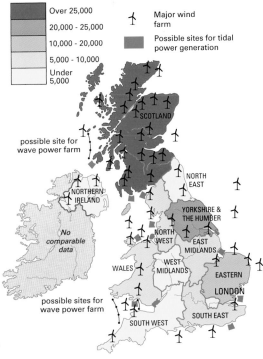

possible site for wave power farm

SCOTLAND

NORTHERN IRELAND

No comparable data

NORTH EAST
YORKSHIRE & THE HUMBER
NORTH WEST
EAST MIDLANDS
WALES
WEST MIDLANDS
EASTERN
LONDON
SOUTH EAST
SOUTH WEST

possible sites for wave power farm

ENERGY SOURCES

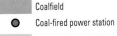

Coalfield
Coal-fired power station
Peat-cutting area in Ireland
Peat-fired power station
Oilfield
Oil pipeline (with terminal)
Oil-fired power station
Gasfield
Gas pipeline (with terminal)
Gas-fired power station
Coal, biomass & gas-fired power station
Hydro-electric power station
Nuclear power station
Only major power stations and fields are shown
International dividing line

ENERGY IMPORTS

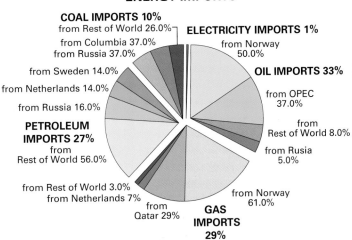

COAL IMPORTS 10%
from Rest of World 26.0%
from Columbia 37.0%
from Russia 37.0%

ELECTRICITY IMPORTS 1%
from Norway 50.0%

from Sweden 14.0%
from Netherlands 14.0%
from Russia 16.0%

OIL IMPORTS 33%
from OPEC 37.0%
from Rest of World 8.0%
from Rusia 5.0%
from Norway 61.0%

PETROLEUM IMPORTS 27%
from Rest of World 56.0%

from Rest of World 3.0%
from Netherlands 7%
from Qatar 29%

GAS IMPORTS 29%

Total U.K. imports 2017 147.9 million tonnes of oil equivalent
Pie chart figures 2015

CHANGES TO COAL MINING IN THE U.K.

	1960	1980	2010	2017
Production (million tonnes)	195	126	18	3
Number of employees (thousands)	631	297	9	1
Number of deep mines	698	211	12	0
Open cast			13	9

Numbers employed

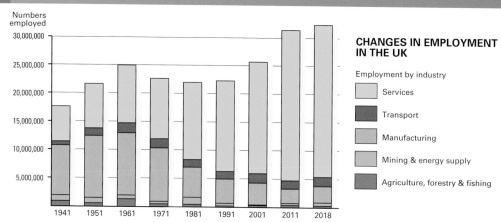

CHANGES IN EMPLOYMENT IN THE UK

Employment by industry

- Services
- Transport
- Manufacturing
- Mining & energy supply
- Agriculture, forestry & fishing

▲ Canary Wharf, London, is a centre of banking – an important part of the service industry.

▲ These Mini Clubman cars are being manufactured at the BMW factory, Oxford.

▲ An engineer is shown working on a jet engine in the Rolls-Royce factory, Derby.

INCOME

The average gross weekly earnings of males and females in full employment in 2017

- Over £600
- £550 – £600
- £525 – £550
- £510 – £525
- £500 – £510

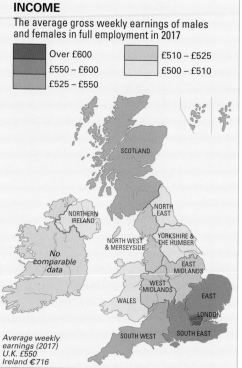

Average weekly earnings (2017)
U.K. £550
Ireland €716

EMPLOYMENT IN SERVICES

The percentage of the workforce employed in the service industry in 2017

- Over 90%
- 85 – 90%
- 80 – 85%
- 75 – 80%
- Under 75%

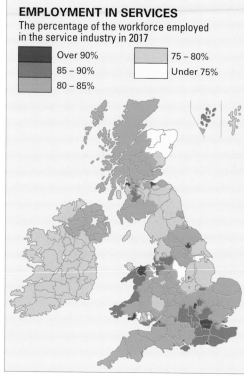

EMPLOYMENT IN MANUFACTURING INDUSTRY

The percentage of the workforce employed in manufacturing in 2017

- Over 15%
- 12.5 – 15%
- 10 – 12.5%
- 7.5 – 10%
- 5 – 7.5%
- Under 5%

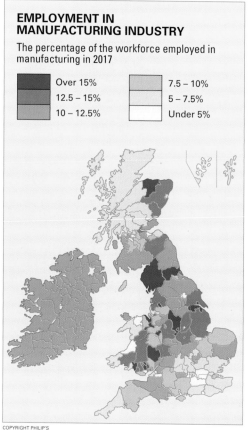

UNEMPLOYMENT

The percentage of the workforce unemployed in 2018

- Over 5%
- 4 – 4%
- 3 – 4%
- Under 3%

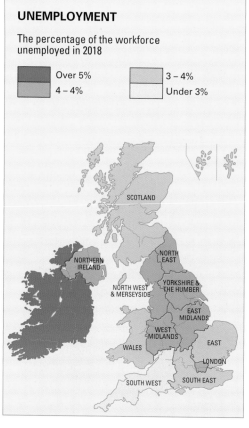

U.K. TRADE

Trade is balanced by money coming in for services such as banking and insurance.

Total Imports 2017
£489.1 billion

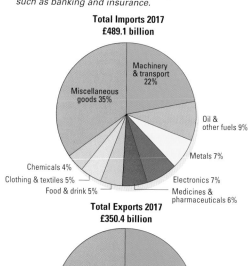

- Machinery & transport 22%
- Miscellaneous goods 35%
- Oil & other fuels 9%
- Metals 7%
- Electronics 7%
- Medicines & pharmaceuticals 6%
- Food & drink 5%
- Clothing & textiles 5%
- Chemicals 4%

Total Exports 2017
£350.4 billion

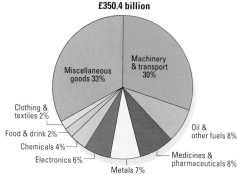

- Machinery & transport 30%
- Miscellaneous goods 33%
- Clothing & textiles 2%
- Food & drink 2%
- Chemicals 4%
- Electronics 6%
- Metals 7%
- Medicines & pharmaceuticals 8%
- Oil & other fuels 8%

POPULATION FACTS

U.K. Population 2017	**66,040,200**
of which England	55,619,400
Scotland	5,424,800
Wales	3,125,200
Northern Ireland	1,870,800
Ireland Population 2017	**5,068,050**

AGE STRUCTURE OF THE U.K. IN 1901 AND 2017

The age structure shows how old people are and the percentage in each age group that is male and female. Each diagram is called a population pyramid. For example, in 1901, 20% of the female population was aged between 10–19. In 2017, about 11% were in this group.

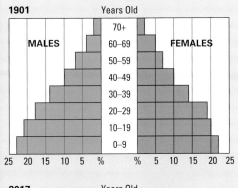

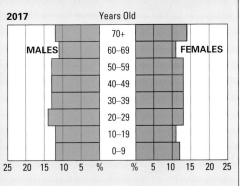

POPULATION DENSITY

Number of people per square kilometre in 2017

- Over 1000
- 500 – 1000
- 200 – 500
- 100 – 200
- 50 – 100
- 25 – 50
- Under 25

The average density for the U.K. is 273 people per km².

The average density for Ireland is 69 people per km².

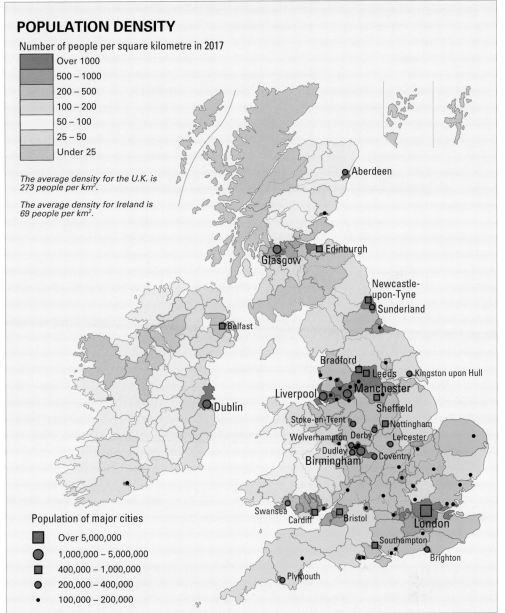

Population of major cities

- Over 5,000,000
- 1,000,000 – 5,000,000
- 400,000 – 1,000,000
- 200,000 – 400,000
- 100,000 – 200,000

NATIONALITY

Non-British as a percentage of total population in 2017

- Over 20%
- 10 – 20%
- 5 – 10%
- 0 – 5%

378 000 Total number of non-British people in each region

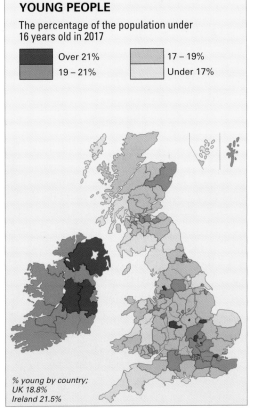

No comparable data

SCOTLAND 378 000
NORTHERN IRELAND 124 000
NORTH EAST 105 000
YORKSHIRE & THE HUMBER 374 000
NORTH WEST & MERSEYSIDE 469 000
EAST MIDLANDS 426 000
WALES 135 000
WEST MIDLANDS 514 000
EAST 507 000
LONDON 2 109 000
SOUTH WEST 321 000
SOUTH EAST 744 000

9.5% of total population are non-British

YOUNG PEOPLE

The percentage of the population under 16 years old in 2017

- Over 21%
- 19 – 21%
- 17 – 19%
- Under 17%

% young by country;
UK 18.8%
Ireland 21.5%

OLDER PEOPLE

The percentage of the population aged 65 and over in 2017

- Over 22%
- 20 – 22%
- 18 – 20%
- 16 – 18%
- 14 – 16%
- Under 14%

% older by country;
UK 18.2%
Ireland 13.4%

ROADS AND FERRIES

Motorways
Other main roads
Principal car ferry routes
Channel Tunnel

RAILWAYS

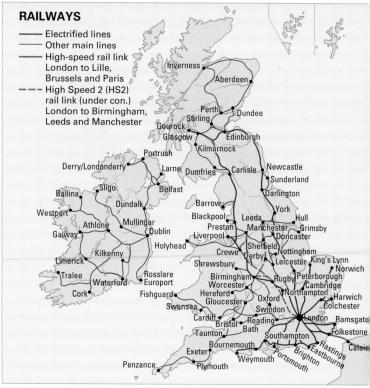

Electrified lines
Other main lines
High-speed rail link London to Lille, Brussels and Paris
High Speed 2 (HS2) rail link (under con.) London to Birmingham, Leeds and Manchester

AIRPORTS

Passenger traffic in millions (2017)

70,000
35,000
10,000
5,000
1,000

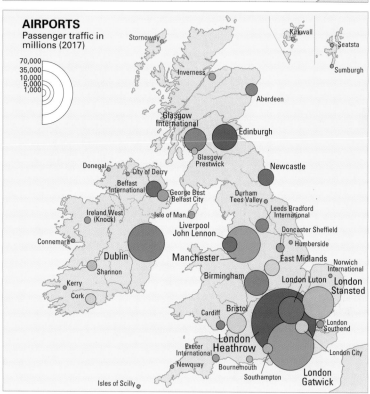

SEAPORTS

Goods traffic by port in million tonnes (2017)

60,000
30,000
10,000
5,000

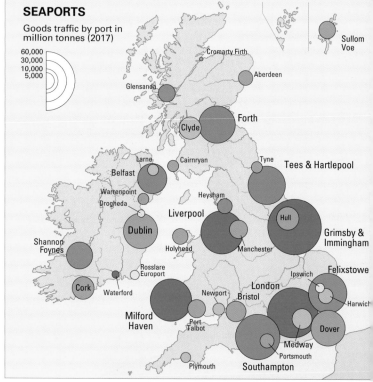

VISITS TO AND FROM THE U.K.

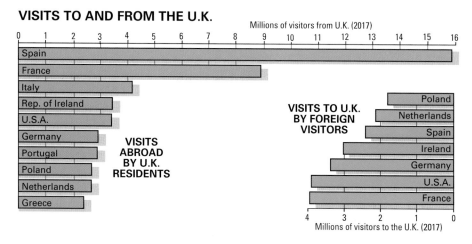

Millions of visitors from U.K. (2017)

| | 0 | 1 | 2 | 3 | 4 | 5 | 6 | 7 | 8 | 9 | 10 | 11 | 12 | 13 | 14 | 15 | 16 |

Spain
France
Italy
Rep. of Ireland
U.S.A.
Germany
Portugal
Poland
Netherlands
Greece

VISITS ABROAD BY U.K. RESIDENTS

VISITS TO U.K. BY FOREIGN VISITORS

Poland
Netherlands
Spain
Ireland
Germany
U.S.A.
France

Millions of visitors to the U.K. (2017)

▲ Eurostar at St. Pancras International. This station is the London terminus of the high-speed rail link to Europe, High Speed 1.

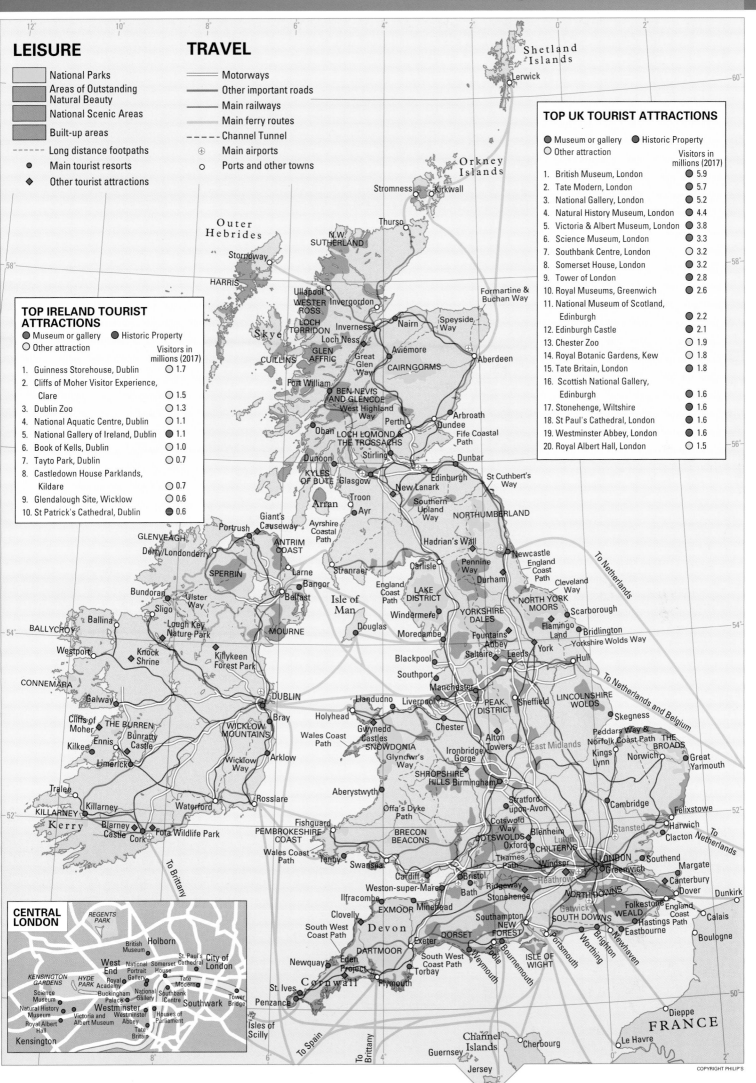

LEISURE

- National Parks
- Areas of Outstanding Natural Beauty
- National Scenic Areas
- Built-up areas
- - - - - Long distance footpaths
- ● Main tourist resorts
- ◆ Other tourist attractions

TRAVEL

- Motorways
- Other important roads
- Main railways
- Main ferry routes
- - - - - Channel Tunnel
- ✈ Main airports
- ○ Ports and other towns

TOP UK TOURIST ATTRACTIONS

● Museum or gallery   ● Historic Property
○ Other attraction

Visitors in millions (2017)

1.	British Museum, London	● 5.9
2.	Tate Modern, London	● 5.7
3.	National Gallery, London	● 5.2
4.	Natural History Museum, London	● 4.4
5.	Victoria & Albert Museum, London	● 3.8
6.	Science Museum, London	● 3.3
7.	Southbank Centre, London	○ 3.2
8.	Somerset House, London	● 3.2
9.	Tower of London	● 2.8
10.	Royal Museums, Greenwich	● 2.6
11.	National Museum of Scotland, Edinburgh	● 2.2
12.	Edinburgh Castle	● 2.1
13.	Chester Zoo	○ 1.9
14.	Royal Botanic Gardens, Kew	○ 1.8
15.	Tate Britain, London	● 1.8
16.	Scottish National Gallery, Edinburgh	● 1.6
17.	Stonehenge, Wiltshire	● 1.6
18.	St Paul's Cathedral, London	● 1.6
19.	Westminster Abbey, London	● 1.6
20.	Royal Albert Hall, London	○ 1.5

TOP IRELAND TOURIST ATTRACTIONS

● Museum or gallery   ● Historic Property
○ Other attraction

Visitors in millions (2017)

1.	Guinness Storehouse, Dublin	○ 1.7
2.	Cliffs of Moher Visitor Experience, Clare	○ 1.5
3.	Dublin Zoo	○ 1.3
4.	National Aquatic Centre, Dublin	○ 1.1
5.	National Gallery of Ireland, Dublin	● 1.1
6.	Book of Kells, Dublin	○ 1.0
7.	Tayto Park, Dublin	○ 0.7
8.	Castledown House Parklands, Kildare	○ 0.7
9.	Glendalough Site, Wicklow	○ 0.6
10.	St Patrick's Cathedral, Dublin	● 0.6

CENTRAL LONDON

COPYRIGHT PHILIP'S

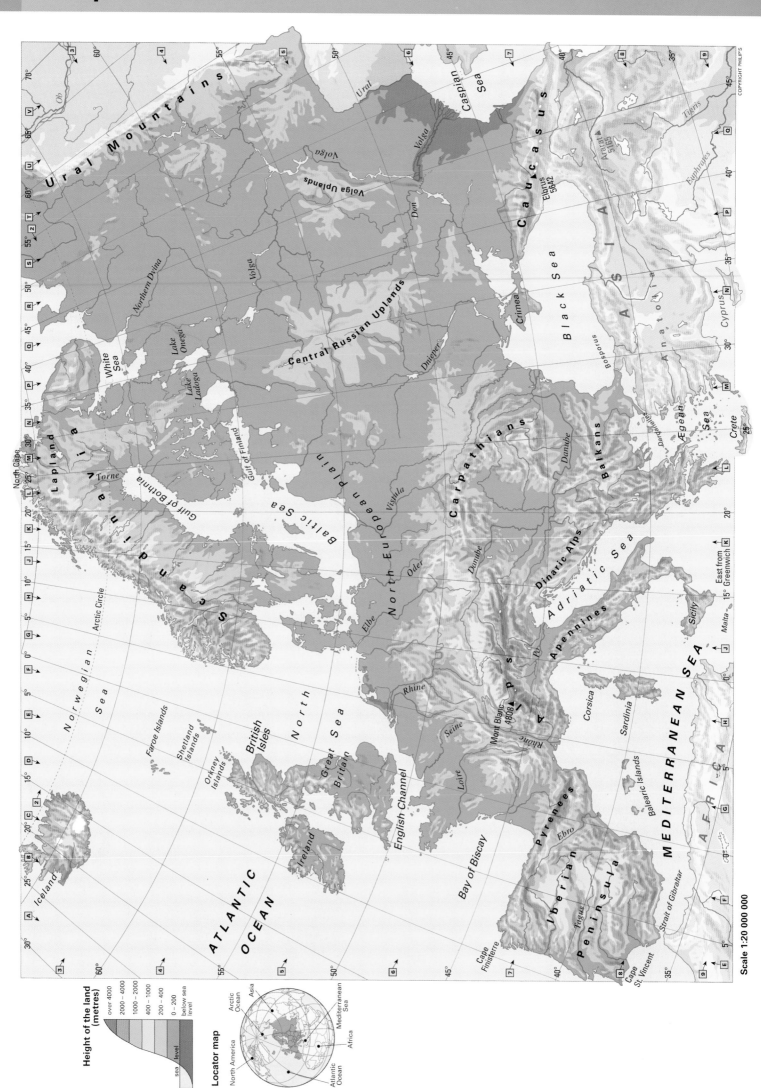

Height of the land
(metres)

over 4000
2000 – 4000
1000 – 2000
400 – 1000
200 – 400
0 – 200
below sea
level

sea level

Locator map

Arctic Ocean
Asia
North America
Atlantic Ocean
Mediterranean Sea
Africa

Scale 1:20 000 000

COPYRIGHT PHILIP'S

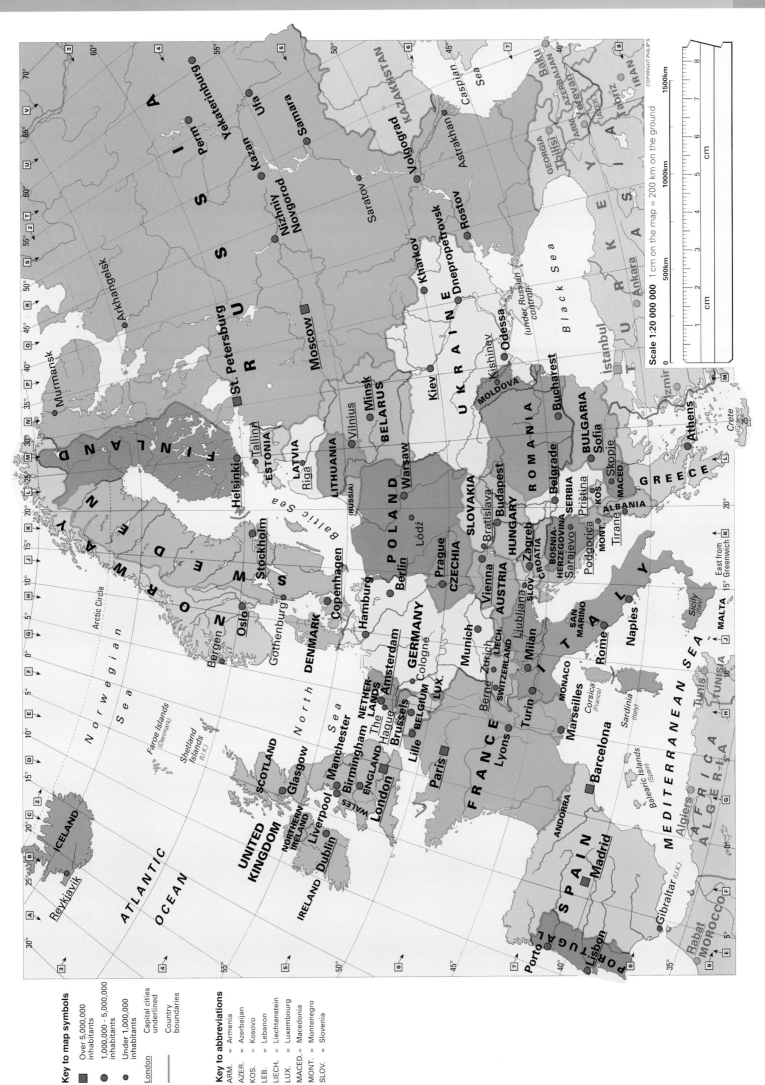

Key to map symbols

■ Over 5,000,000 inhabitants

● 1,000,000 - 5,000,000 inhabitants

• Under 1,000,000 inhabitants

London Capital cities underlined

Country boundaries

Key to abbreviations

ARM. = Armenia
AZER. = Azerbaijan
KOS. = Kosovo
LEB. = Lebanon
LIECH. = Liechtenstein
LUX. = Luxembourg
MACED. = Macedonia
MONT. = Montenegro
SLOV. = Slovenia

Scale 1:20 000 000 1 cm on the map = 200 km on the ground

COPYRIGHT PHILIP'S

0   500km   1000km   1500km

EUROPEAN UNION

This map shows the members of the European Union and the year that they joined.

- Founder members (Treaty of Rome 1957)
- Joined in 1973
- Joined in 1981
- Joined in 1986
- Joined in 1990 (German unification)
- Joined in 1995
- Joined in 2004
- Joined in 2007
- Joined in 2013

The UK plans to leave the EU in 2019

- ○ HQ of European institutions
- € Euro-zone
- Non-members

Albania, Macedonia, Montenegro, Serbia and Turkey have applied for membership of the EU

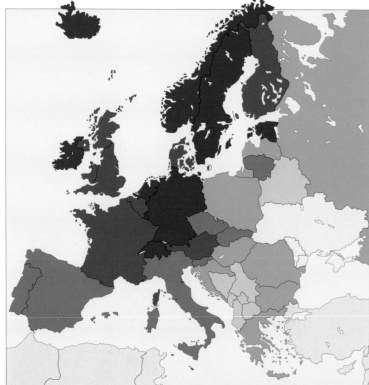

WEALTH

The value of total production divided by population (US $, 2017)

- Over $50,000 per person
- $40,000 – 50,000 per person
- $30,000 – 40,000 per person
- $20,000 – 30,000 per person
- $10,000 – 20,000 per person
- Under $10,000 per person

Wealthiest countries:
Liechtenstein US$139,100
Monaco US$115,700
Luxembourg US$109,100

Poorest countries:
Moldova US$5,700
Ukraine US$8,700
Kosovo US$10,400

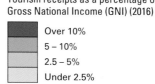

COPYRIGHT PHILIP'S

TOURISM

Tourism receipts as a percentage of Gross National Income (GNI) (2016)

- Over 10%
- 5 – 10%
- 2.5 – 5%
- Under 2.5%

Tourist destinations

- ■ Cultural & historical centres
- ☐ Coastal resorts
- ☐ Ski resorts
- ■ Centres of entertainment
- ■ Places of pilgrimage
- ■ Places of great natural beauty

Scale 1:10 000 000 1 cm on the map = 100 km on the ground

0 100km 200km 300km 400km 500km 600km

Height of the land (metres)

over 4000
2000–4000
1000–2000
400–1000
200–400
0–200
sea level
below sea level

Key to map symbols

■ Over 5,000,000 inhabitants

● 1,000,000 – 5,000,000 inhabitants

● Under 1,000,000 inhabitants

Helsinki Capital cities underlined

—— Country boundaries

Locator map

COPYRIGHT PHILIP'S

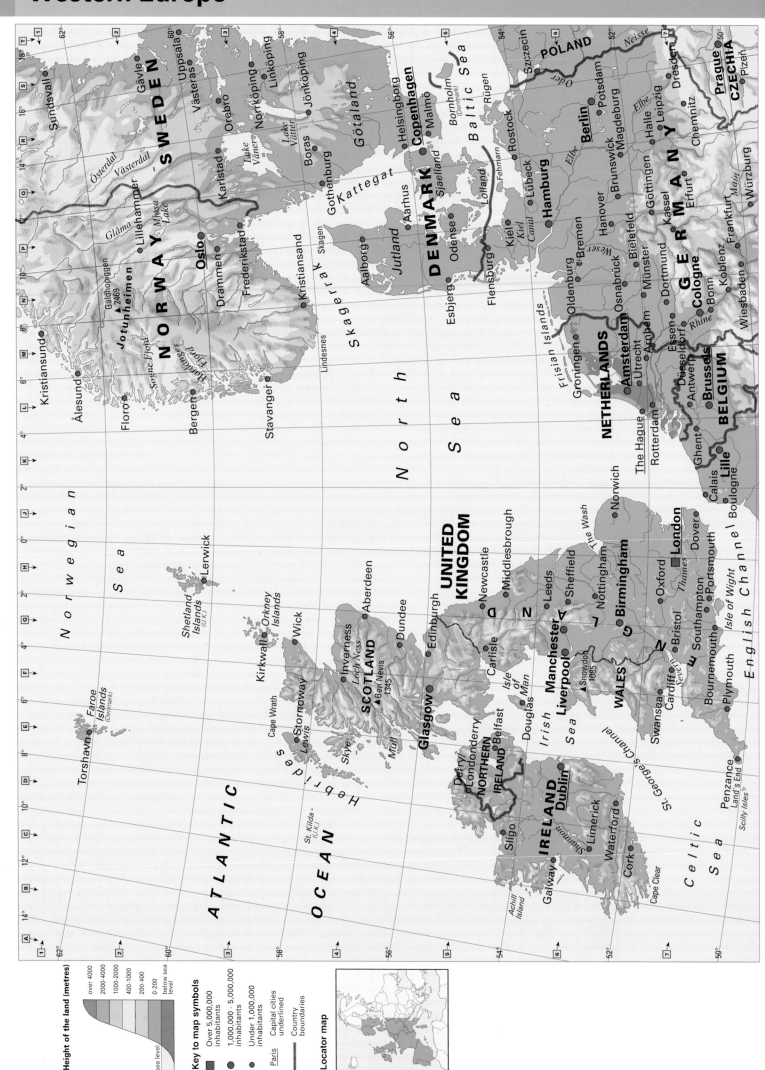

Height of the land (metres)

over 4000
2000-4000
1000-2000
400-1000
200-400
0-200
below sea level

sea level

Key to map symbols

● Over 5,000,000 inhabitants
● 1,000,000 - 5,000,000 inhabitants
● Under 1,000,000 inhabitants

Paris Capital cities underlined

Country boundaries

Locator map

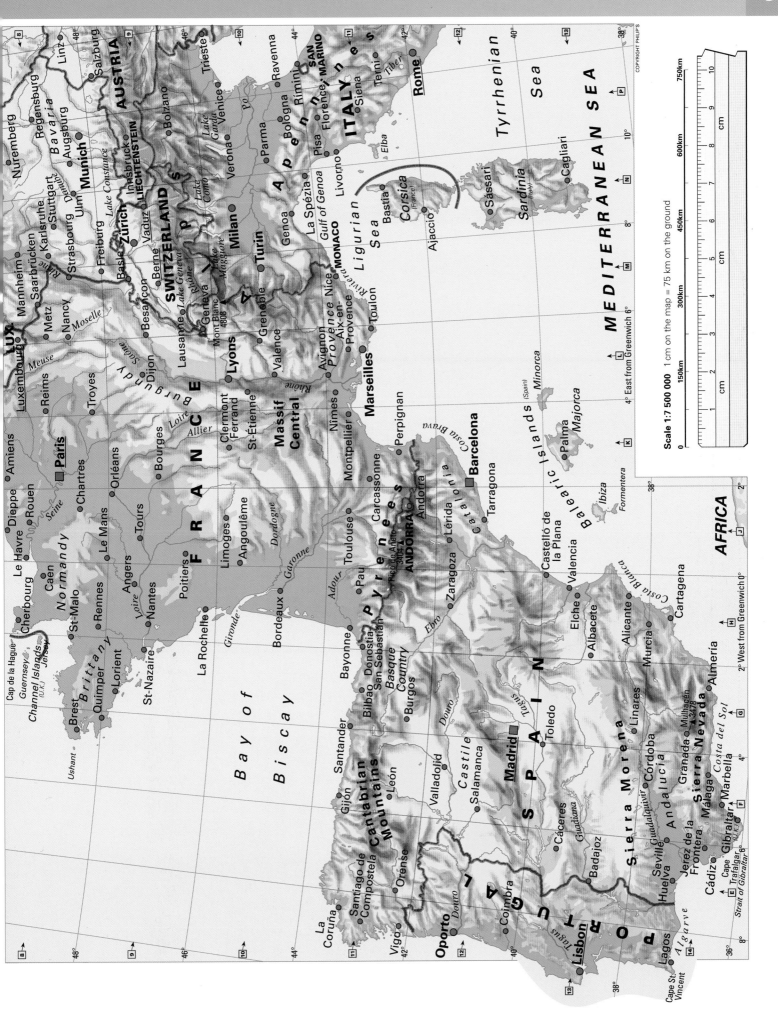

Scale 1:7 500 000 1cm on the map = 75 km on the ground

0   150km   300km   450km   600km   750km

ATLANTIC OCEAN

IRELAND

WALES
Cardiff
Plymouth
Bristol
Birmingham
ENGLAND
London
Thames

Channel Islands (U.K.)
English Channel
Brest

NETHERLANDS
The Hague
Amsterdam
Rotterdam
Antwerp
LUXEMBOURG
Luxembourg
BELGIUM
Brussels
Lille
Le Havre

Hamburg
Szczecin
Bremen
Hanover
Berlin
Oder
Elbe
GERMANY
Dortmund
Cologne
Bonn
Leipzig
Dresden
Frankfurt
Prague
CZECHIA
Mannheim
Nuremberg
Stuttgart

Bay of Biscay

FRANCE
Paris
Seine
Rennes
Nantes
Loire
Orléans
Tours
Dijon
Nancy
Strasbourg
Basle
Rhine
Munich
Linz
AUSTRIA

Limoges
Clermont Ferrand
Lyons
St. Etienne
Massif Central
Garonne
Rhône
Grenoble
Jura
SWITZERLAND
Berne
Geneva
Lake Geneva
Mont Blanc 4808
Milan
Turin
Zürich
LIECHTENSTEIN
Verona
Lake Garda
Ljubliana
SLOVENIA
Trieste
Venice

La Coruña
Vigo
Gijón
Santander
Cantabrian Mountains
León
Bilbao
Burgos
Pyrenees
Pic d'Aneto 3404
ANDORRA
Bordeaux
Toulouse
Montpellier
Marseilles
Toulon
Nice
MONACO
Riviera
Genoa
Parma
Po
Bologna
Florence
Pisa
Siena
Apennines
SAN MARINO
Rímini
Adriatic

PORTUGAL
Oporto
Douro
Salamanca
Valladolid
Douro
SPAIN
Madrid
Tagus
Toledo
Zaragoza
Ebro
Catalonia
Costa Brava
Barcelona
Corsica (France)
Ajaccio
Rome
ITALY
Gran Sasso 2914

Lisbon
Tagus
Badajoz
Guadiana
Sierra Morena
Valencia
Balearic Islands (Spain)
Palma
Majorca
Minorca
Ibiza
Mount Vesuvius 1281
Naples
Pompeii
Sardinia (Italy)

Algarve
Seville
Guadalquivir
Cordoba
Granada
Mulhacén 3478
Murcia
Cartagena
Alicante
Almeria
Costa Blanca
Cágliari
Tyrrhenian Sea
Strómboli

Cádiz
Málaga
Costa del Sol
Gibraltar (U.K.)
Strait of Gibraltar
Ceuta (Spain)
Tangier
Tétouan
Melilla (Spain)
Oujda
Fès
Ifrane
MOROCCO
Atlas Mountains
Palermo
Etna 3340
Sicily
Catánia

Algiers
Blida
Mostaganem
Oran
Bejaïa
Annaba
Constantine
Bizerte
Tunis
Carthage
ALGERIA
Biskra
Sahara
Chott Melrhir
Chott Djerid
TUNISIA
Sousse
Sfax
Djerba
Valletta
MALTA
MEDITERRANEAN

AFRICA
Tripoli
Al Aziziyah
LIBYA

Height of the land (metres)

over 4000	
2000-4000	
1000-2000	
400-1000	
200-400	
0-200	
sea level	
below sea level	

Key to map symbols

Over 5,000,000 inhabitants
1,000,000 - 5,000,000 inhabitants
Under 1,000,000 inhabitants
Sofia Capital cities underlined
Country boundaries
Historical sites   Seasonal lakes

Scale 1:10 000 000   1 cm on the map = 100 km on the ground

0   250km   500km   750km   1000km

1 2 3 4 5 6 7 8 9 10
cm   cm   cm

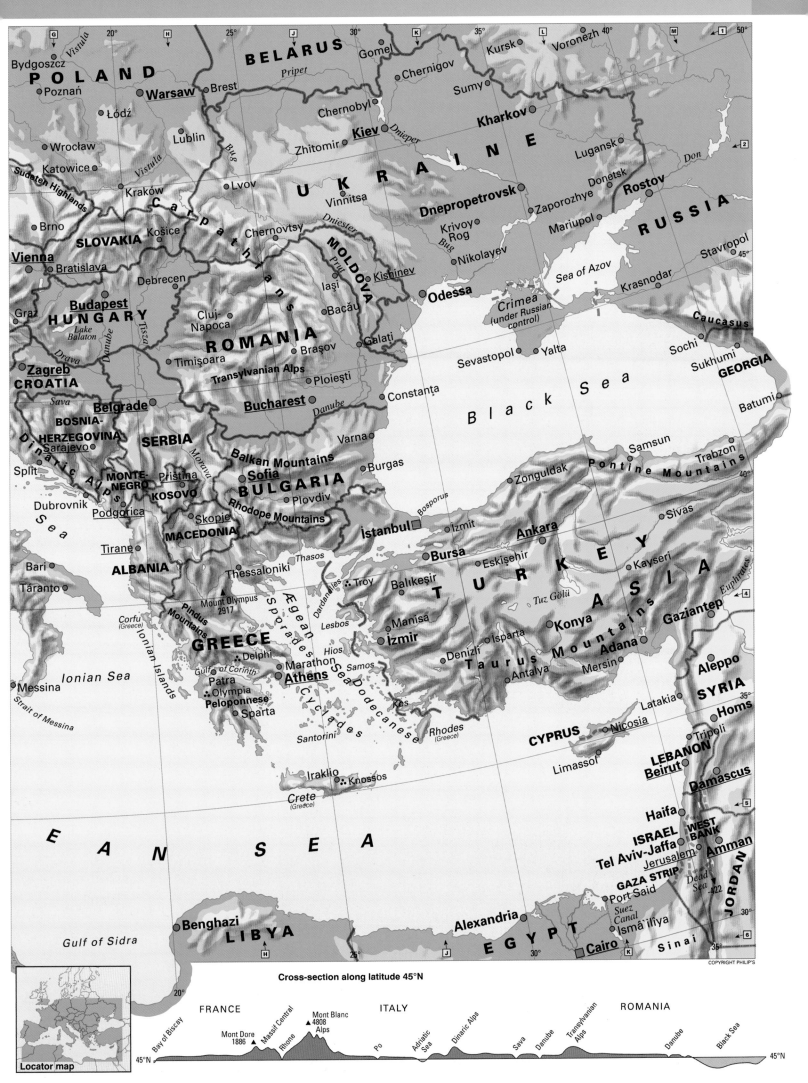

POLAND
Bydgoszcz
Poznań
Łódź
Warsaw
Wrocław
Katowice
Kraków
Brno
SLOVAKIA
Vienna
Bratislava
Graz
Budapest
HUNGARY
Zagreb
CROATIA
BOSNIA-
HERZEGOVINA
Sarajevo
Split
MONTE-
NEGRO
KOSOVO
Dubrovnik
Podgorica
Sea
Tirane
ALBANIA
Bari
Táranto

BELARUS
Gomel
Pripet
Brest
Chernigov
Chernobyl
Kiev
Dnieper
Zhitomir
UKRAINE
Lvov
Vinnitsa
Chernovtsy
Dniester
MOLDOVA
Iaşi
Kishinev
Bacău
ROMANIA
Cluj-
Napoca
Brasov
Timişoara
Transylvanian Alps
Galaţi
Ploieşti
Bucharest
Danube
Varna
Balkan Mountains
SERBIA
Belgrade
Pristina
Sofia
BULGARIA
Plovdiv
Skopje
Rhodope Mountains
MACEDONIA

Kursk
Voronezh
Sumy
Kharkov
Lugansk
Don
Dnepropetrovsk
Donetsk
Rostov
Krivoy
Rog
Zaporozhye
Mariupol
Nikolayev
RUSSIA
Odessa
Crimea
(under Russian
control)
Sea of Azov
Stavropol
Krasnodar
Sevastopol
Yalta
Caucasus
Sochi
Sukhumi
GEORGIA
Black Sea
Batumi

Constanţa
Samsun
Trabzon
Zonguldak
Pontine Mountains
Sivas
Istanbul
Izmit
Ankara
Eskişehir
Kayseri
Bursa
TURKEY
Balıkesir
Troy
Dardanelles
ASIA
Tuz Gölü
Manisa
Konya
Gaziantep
İzmir
Isparta
Taurus Mountains
Adana
Denizli
Mersin
Antalya
Aleppo
SYRIA
Latakia
Homs
CYPRUS
Nicosia
Tripoli
Limassol
LEBANON
Beirut
Damascus
Haifa
ISRAEL
WEST
BANK
Tel Aviv-Jaffa
Jerusalem
Amman
GAZA STRIP
Port Said
Dead
Sea
Suez
Canal
Ismâ`îliya
JORDAN

Thessaloniki
Thasos
Mount Olympus
2917
Sporades
Pindus
Mountains
Corfu
(Greece)
Ionian Islands
GREECE
Aegean
Lesbos
Delphi
Hios
Marathon
Gulf of Corinth
Samos
Patra
Athens
Olympia
Sea
Dodecanese
Peloponnese
Cyclades
Sparta
Kos
Santorini
Rhodes
(Greece)
Iraklio
Knossos
Crete
(Greece)

Messina
Strait of Messina
Ionian Sea

E   A   N   S   E   A

Benghazi
Gulf of Sidra
LIBYA
Alexandria
EGYPT
Cairo
Sinai
Port Said
Ismâ`îliya

Cross-section along latitude 45°N

FRANCE   ITALY   ROMANIA

Bay of Biscay
Mont Dore
1886
Massif Central
Mont Blanc
4808
Alps
Rhone
Po
Adriatic Sea
Dinaric Alps
Sava
Danube
Transylvanian
Alps
Danube
Black Sea
45°N   45°N

Locator map

COPYRIGHT PHILIP'S

SWITZERLAND

Mont Blanc
46 4808 ▲

Monte Rosa
4634

A l p s

Dolomites

Bolzano
3342 ▲
Trento
Údine
Trieste

SLOVENIA

AUSTRIA

CROATIA

Lake Maggiore
Lake Como
Lake Garda

Milan
Novara
Brescia
Bergamo
Vicenza
Verona
Padua
Venice

Turin
Piacenza
Alessandria
Parma
Réggio
Módena
Bologna
Ferrara
Ravenna
SAN MARINO
Rímini

Genoa
Gulf of Genoa
La Spézia
Florence
Forli
Ancona

Riviera
San Remo
MONACO
Pisa
Livorno
Siena
Perúgia
Terni
2912 ▲
Pescara

Ligurian Sea
Elba
Grosseto

Corsica (France)

Celano

VATICAN CITY
Rome
Latina
Fóggia
Bari

Strait of Bonifacio

Ólbia

Sássari

Mount Vesuvius
1281 ▲
Naples
Pompeii
Ischia
Salerno
Capri
Sorrento
Potenza
Táranto
Brindisi
Lecce

Sardinia (Italy)
1834 ▲

Gulf of Táranto

Strait of Otranto

Tyrrhenian Sea

Cosenza
1928 ▲

Ionian Sea

Cágliari

Strómboli
924 ▲
Aeolian Islands

Messina
Réggio di Calabria

Locator map

Égadi Islands
Palermo
Marsala
Mount Etna
3323 ▲
Sicily

Catánia
Pantelleria
Siracusa

East from Greenwich

A t l a n t i c

A p e n n i n e s

Po
Tiber

A d r i a t i c   S e a

▲ **Strómboli** Known as the 'Lighthouse of the Mediterranean', it is one of three active volcanoes in Italy. The others are Mount Etna and Mount Vesuvius.

Scale 1:6 250 000   1 cm on the map = 62.5 km on the ground

| 0 | 62.5km | 125km | 187.5km | 250km | 312.5km | 375km |

cm

Key to map symbols

■ Over 1,000,000 inhabitants

● 500,000 – 1,000,000 inhabitants

● Under 500,000 inhabitants

Rome Capital cities

━━ Country boundaries

⸫ Historical site

Height of the land (metres)

over 4000
2000-4000
1000-2000
400-1000
200-400
0-200
below sea level

sea level

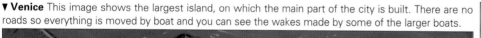

▼ **Venice** This image shows the largest island, on which the main part of the city is built. There are no roads so everything is moved by boat and you can see the wakes made by some of the larger boats.

REGIONS

VALLE D'AOSTA
ALTO ADIGE TRENTINO
LOMBARDY
FRIULI-VENEZIA GIULIA
PIEDMONT
VENETO
LIGURIA
EMILIA-ROMAGNA
TUSCANY
MARCHE
UMBRIA
ABRUZZO
LAZIO
MOLISE
SARDINIA
CAMPANIA
PUGLIA
BASILICATA
CALABRIA
SICILY

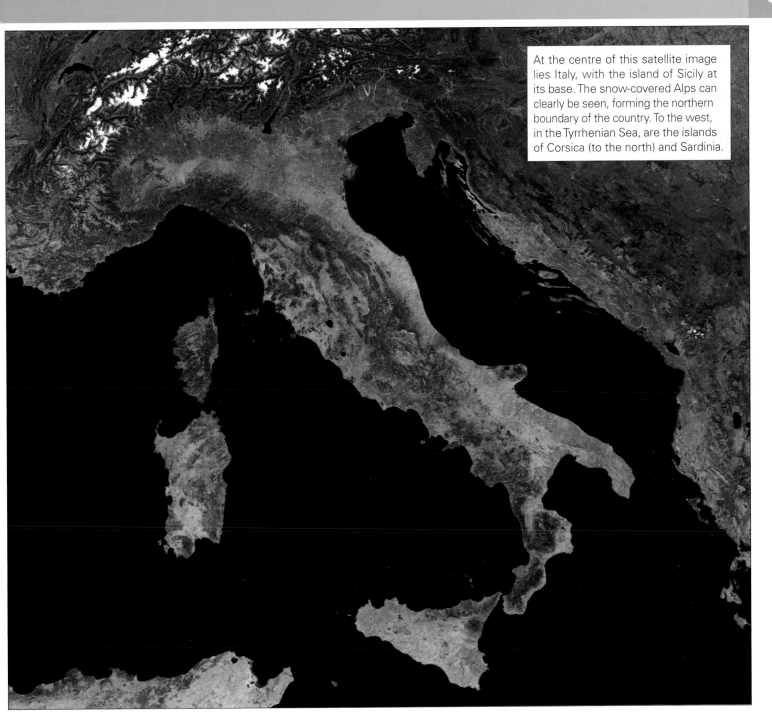

At the centre of this satellite image lies Italy, with the island of Sicily at its base. The snow-covered Alps can clearly be seen, forming the northern boundary of the country. To the west, in the Tyrrhenian Sea, are the islands of Corsica (to the north) and Sardinia.

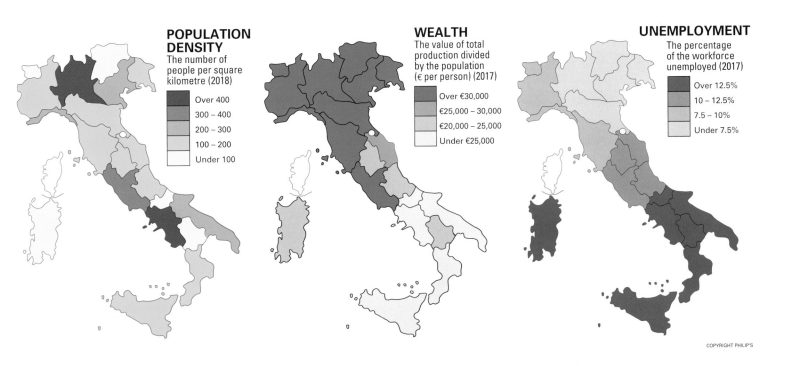

POPULATION DENSITY

The number of people per square kilometre (2018)

- Over 400
- 300 – 400
- 200 – 300
- 100 – 200
- Under 100

WEALTH

The value of total production divided by the population (€ per person) (2017)

- Over €30,000
- €25,000 – 30,000
- €20,000 – 25,000
- Under €25,000

UNEMPLOYMENT

The percentage of the workforce unemployed (2017)

- Over 12.5%
- 10 – 12.5%
- 7.5 – 10%
- Under 7.5%

Height of the land (metres)

over 4000
3000-4000
2000-3000
1000-2000
400-1000
200-400
0-200
below sea level

sea level

Locator map

North America
Arctic Ocean
Pacific Ocean
Oceania
Europe
Asia
Africa
Indian Ocean

Scale 1:48 000 000

COPYRIGHT PHILIPS

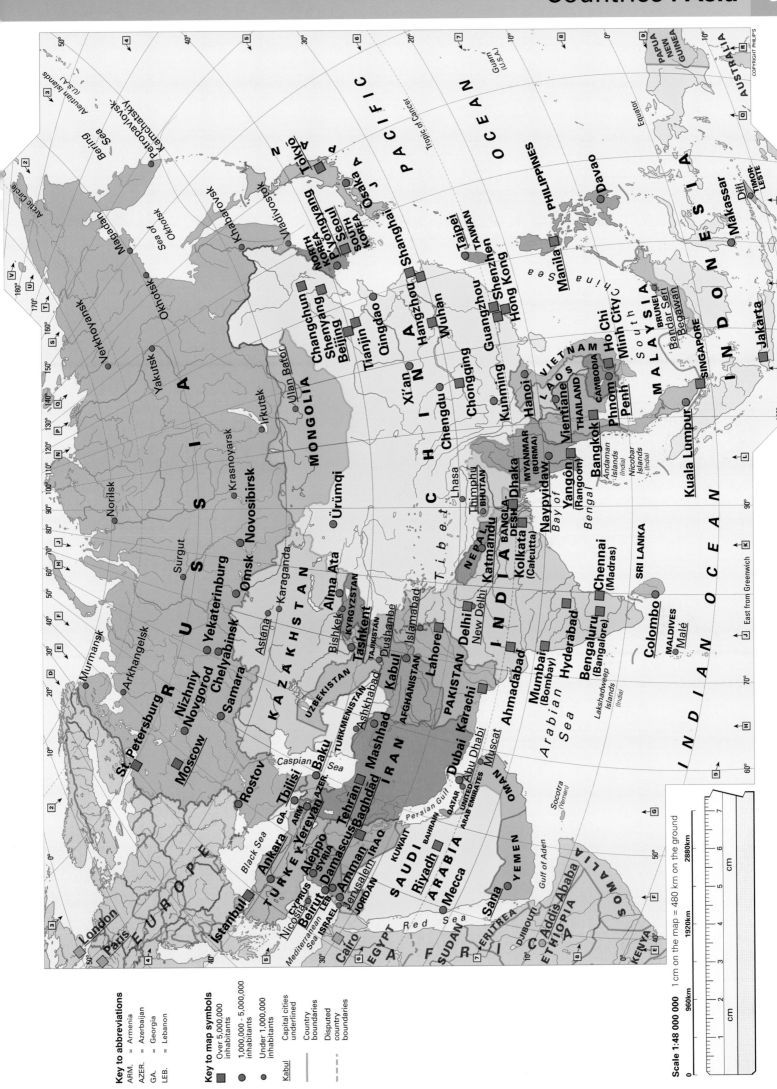

Key to abbreviations
ARM. = Armenia
AZER. = Azerbaijan
GA. = Georgia
LEB. = Lebanon

Key to map symbols
■ Over 5,000,000 inhabitants
● 1,000,000 - 5,000,000 inhabitants
• Under 1,000,000 inhabitants
Kabul Capital cities underlined
—— Country boundaries
- - - Disputed country boundaries

Scale 1:48 000 000   1 cm on the map = 480 km on the ground
0   960km   1920km   2880km

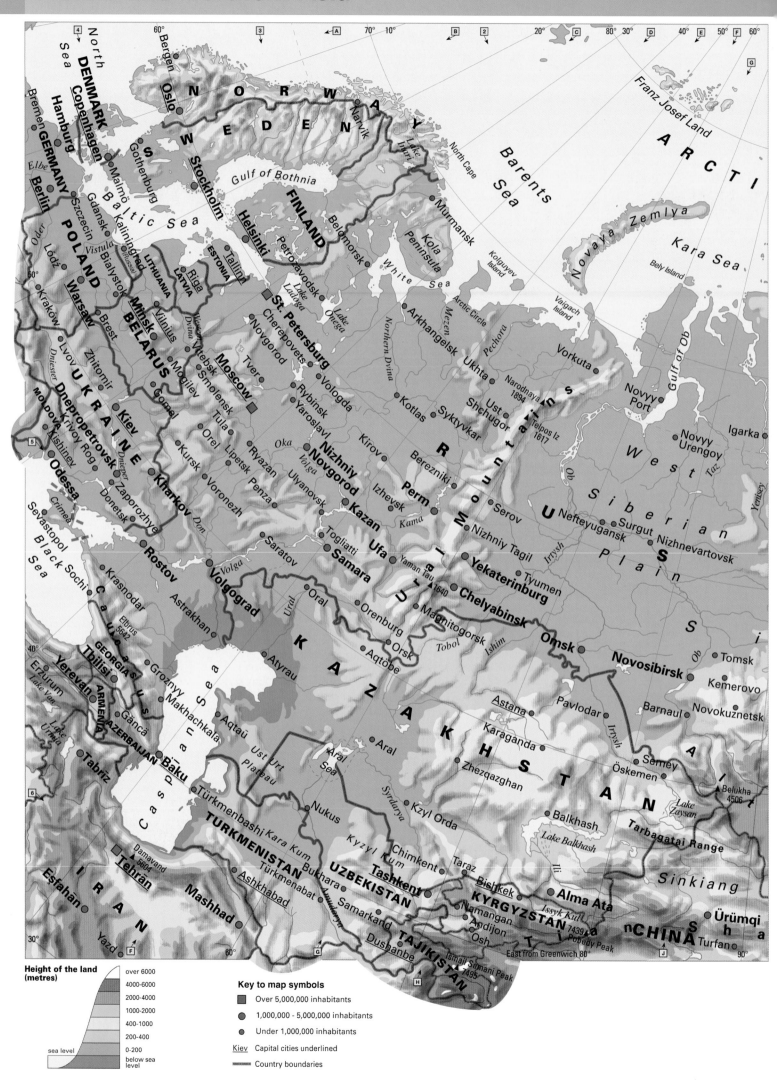

**Height of the land
(metres)**

	over 6000
	4000-6000
	2000-4000
	1000-2000
	400-1000
	200-400
	0-200
sea level	below sea level

Key to map symbols

◼ Over 5,000,000 inhabitants

● 1,000,000 - 5,000,000 inhabitants

• Under 1,000,000 inhabitants

<u>Kiev</u> Capital cities underlined

━━━ Country boundaries

Scale 1:20 000 000   1 cm on the map = 200 km on the ground

| 0 | 500km | 1000km | 1500km | 2000km | 2500km |

Locator map

COPYRIGHT PHILIP'S

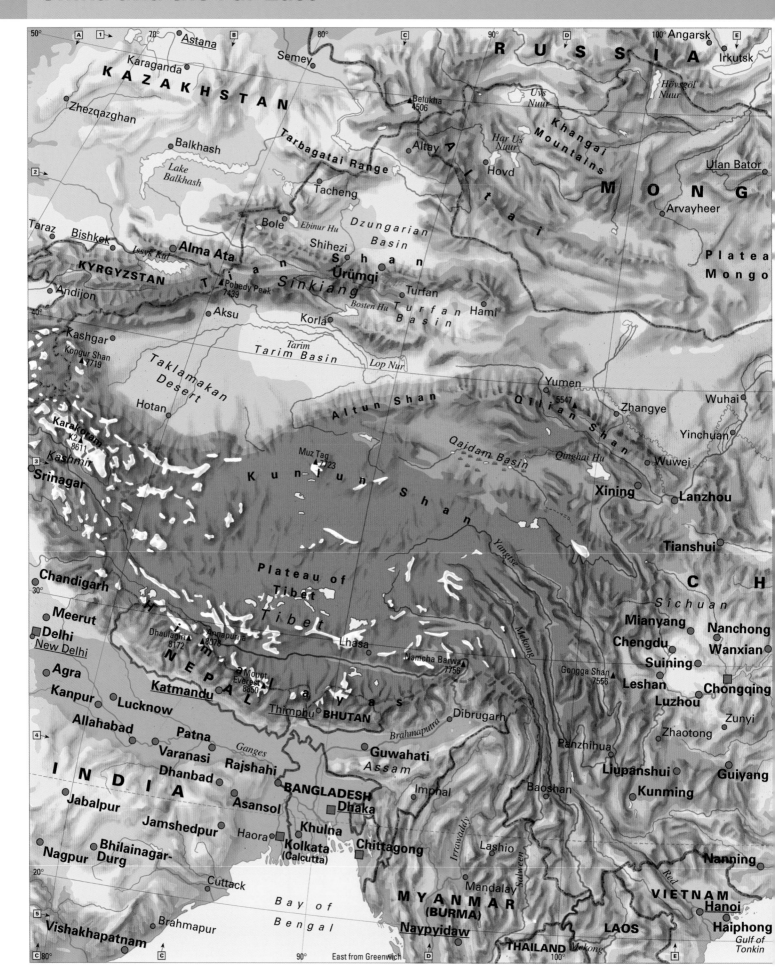

KAZAKHSTAN

Astana
Karaganda
Semey
Zhezqazghan

RUSSIA
Angarsk
Irkutsk

Balkhash
Tarbagatai Range
Belukha 4506
Uvs Nuur
Har Us Nuur
Khangai Mountains
Hövsgöl Nuur

Lake Balkhash
Altay
Hovd
Ulan Bator

Taraz
Bishkek
Alma Ata
Tacheng
Bole
Ebinur Hu
Dzungarian Basin
Shihezi
Ürümqi
Turfan
Arvayheer

MONGO

Platea Mongo

KYRGYZSTAN
Andijan
Issyk Kul
Tian Shan
Sinkiang
Pobedy Peak 7439
Turfan Basin
Hami

Aksu
Korla
Bosten Hu
Lop Nur

Kashgar
Kongur Shan 7719
Tarim Basin
Tarim
Yumen
5547
Zhangye
Wuhai
Yinchuan

Taklamakan Desert
Hotan
Altun Shan
Qilian Shan
Qaidam Basin
Wuwei

Karakoram
K2 8611
Muz Tag 7723
Qinghai Hu
Xining
Lanzhou

Kashmir
Srinagar
Kun lun Shan

Chandigarh
Plateau of Tibet
Yangtse
Tianshui

Meerut
Tibet
Lhasa
Mekong
CH

Delhi
New Delhi
Dhaulagiri 8172
Annapurna 8078
Namcha Barwa 7756
Sichuan
Mianyang
Nanchong

Agra
NEPAL
Mount Everest 8850
Gongga Shan 7556
Chengdu
Wanxian

Kanpur
Lucknow
Katmandu
Thimphu
BHUTAN
Himalayas
Suining
Leshan
Chongqing
Luzhou

Allahabad
Patna
Ganges
Dibrugarh
Brahmaputra
Panzhihua
Zunyi
Zhaotong

Varanasi
Rajshahi
Guwahati
Assam

INDIA
Dhanbad
BANGLADESH
Impnal
Baoshan
Liupanshui
Guiyang

Jabalpur
Asansol
Dhaka
Kunming

Jamshedpur
Haora
Khulna
Chittagong
Lashio

Nagpur
Bhilainagar-Durg
Kolkata (Calcutta)
Irrawaddy
Mandalay
Salween
Nanning

Cuttack
Brahmapur
Bay of Bengal
MYANMAR (BURMA)
VIETNAM
Hanoi
Haiphong

Vishakhapatnam
Naypyidaw
THAILAND
Mekong
LAOS
Gulf of Tonkin

East from Greenwich

Scale 1:15 000 000   1 cm on the map = 150 km on the ground

0   300km   600km   900km   1200km   1500km

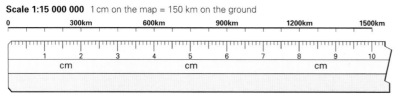

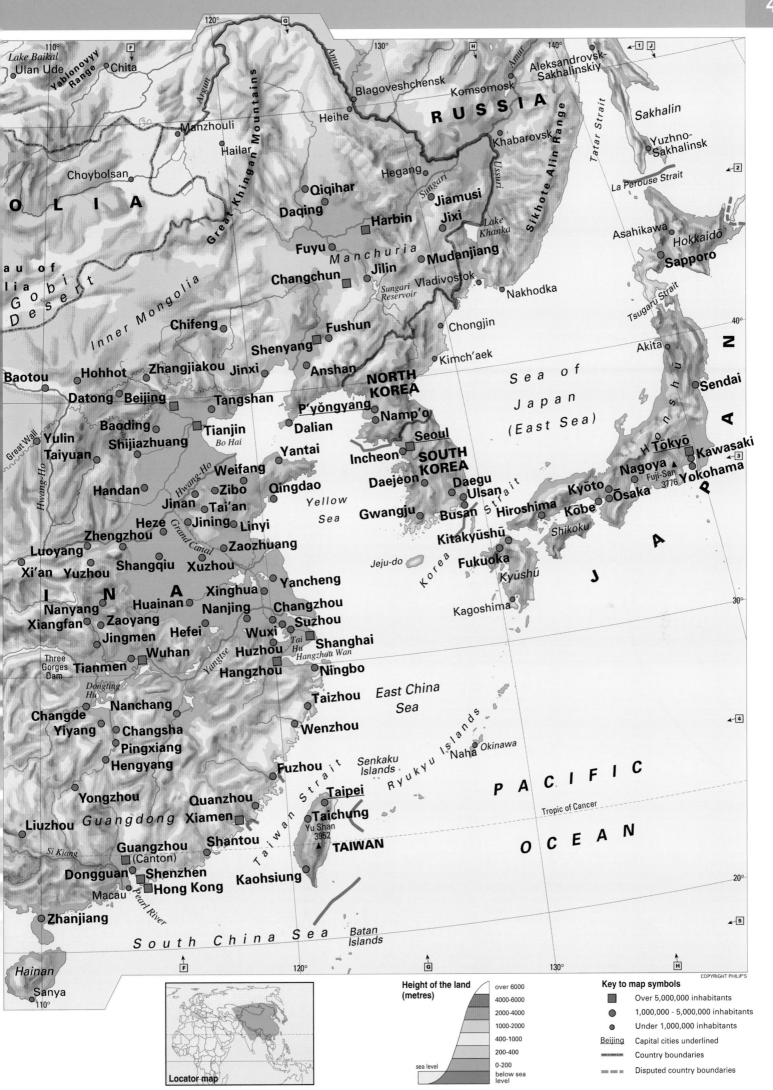

Height of the land (metres)

	over 6000
	4000–6000
	2000–4000
	1000–2000
	400–1000
	200–400
sea level	0–200
	below sea level

Locator map

Key to map symbols

■	Over 5,000,000 inhabitants
●	1,000,000 – 5,000,000 inhabitants
•	Under 1,000,000 inhabitants
<u>Beijing</u>	Capital cities underlined
▄▄▄	Country boundaries
─ ─ ─	Disputed country boundaries

COPYRIGHT PHILIP'S

INDUSTRIAL REGIONS

Core industrial regions

● Major centres for industry

· Centres for iron and steel, and chemicals

Rapidly developing coastal regions

■ Special Economic Zones

▼ Special Administrative Regions

Outer industrial regions

Outer industrial regions with traditional heavy industry

Remote undeveloped regions

← Direction of future growth

— Important rail links

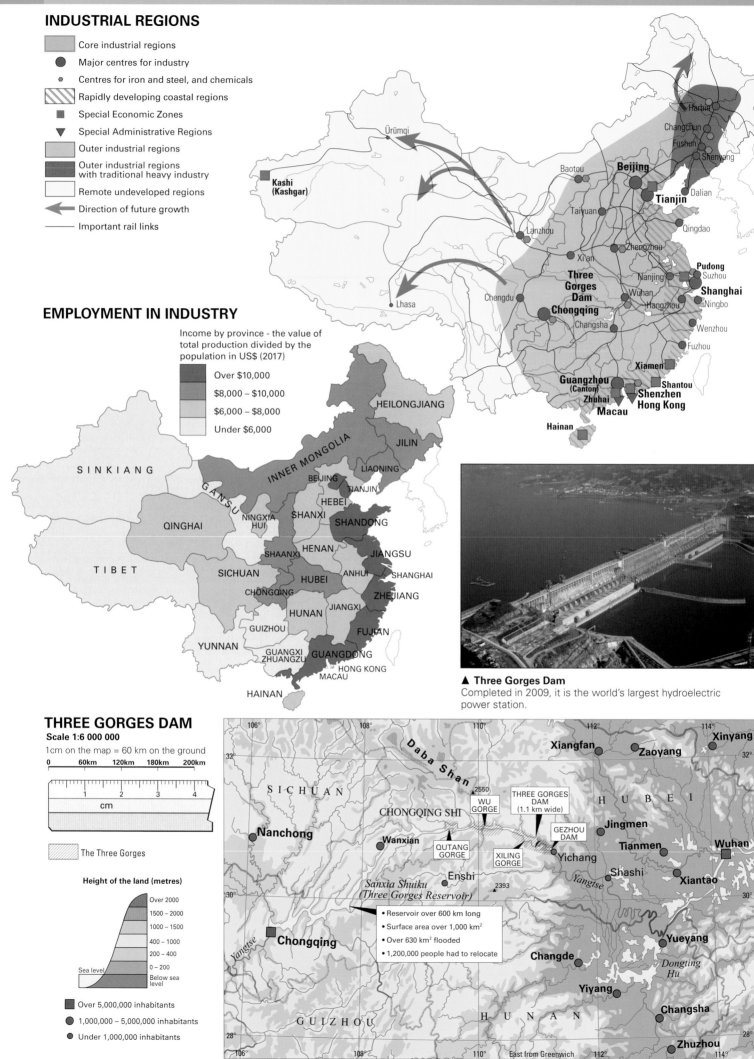

Kashi (Kashgar)

Ürümqi

Baotou

Beijing

Tianjin

Taiyuan

Lanzhou

Dalian

Qingdao

Zhengzhou

Xi'an

Three Gorges Dam

Chongqing

Nanjing

Pudong Suzhou

Shanghai

Wuhan

Hangzhou

Ningbo

Changsha

Wenzhou

Chengdu

Fuzhou

Xiamen

Guangzhou (Canton)

Zhuhai

Shantou

Shenzhen

Macau

Hong Kong

Hainan

Harbin

Changchun

Fushun

Shenyang

Lhasa

EMPLOYMENT IN INDUSTRY

Income by province - the value of total production divided by the population in US$ (2017)

Over $10,000

$8,000 – $10,000

$6,000 – $8,000

Under $6,000

SINKIANG

HEILONGJIANG

JILIN

INNER MONGOLIA

LIAONING

GANSU

BEIJING

NINGXIA HUI

TIANJIN

QINGHAI

SHANXI

HEBEI

SHANDONG

SHAANXI

HENAN

TIBET

JIANGSU

SICHUAN

ANHUI

SHANGHAI

CHONGQING

HUBEI

ZHEJIANG

HUNAN

JIANGXI

GUIZHOU

FUJIAN

YUNNAN

GUANGXI ZHUANGZU

GUANGDONG

HONG KONG MACAU

HAINAN

▲ **Three Gorges Dam**
Completed in 2009, it is the world's largest hydroelectric power station.

THREE GORGES DAM

Scale 1:6 000 000

1cm on the map = 60 km on the ground

0   60km   120km   180km   200km

cm
1   2   3   4

The Three Gorges

Height of the land (metres)

Over 2000

1500 – 2000

1000 – 1500

400 – 1000

200 – 400

0 – 200

Sea level

Below sea level

■ Over 5,000,000 inhabitants

● 1,000,000 – 5,000,000 inhabitants

● Under 1,000,000 inhabitants

SICHUAN

Daba Shan

Xinyang

Xiangfan

Zaoyang

2550

WU GORGE

THREE GORGES DAM (1.1 km wide)

HUBEI

CHONGQING SHI

Jingmen

Nanchong

Wanxian

QUTANG GORGE

XILING GORGE

GEZHOU DAM

Tianmen

Wuhan

Yichang

Shashi

Enshi

2393

Xiantao

Sanxia Shuiku (Three Gorges Reservoir)

Yangtse

• Reservoir over 600 km long
• Surface area over 1,000 km²
• Over 630 km² flooded
• 1,200,000 people had to relocate

Yueyang

Chongqing

Yangtse

Changde

Dongting Hu

Yiyang

Changsha

GUIZHOU

HUNAN

Zhuzhou

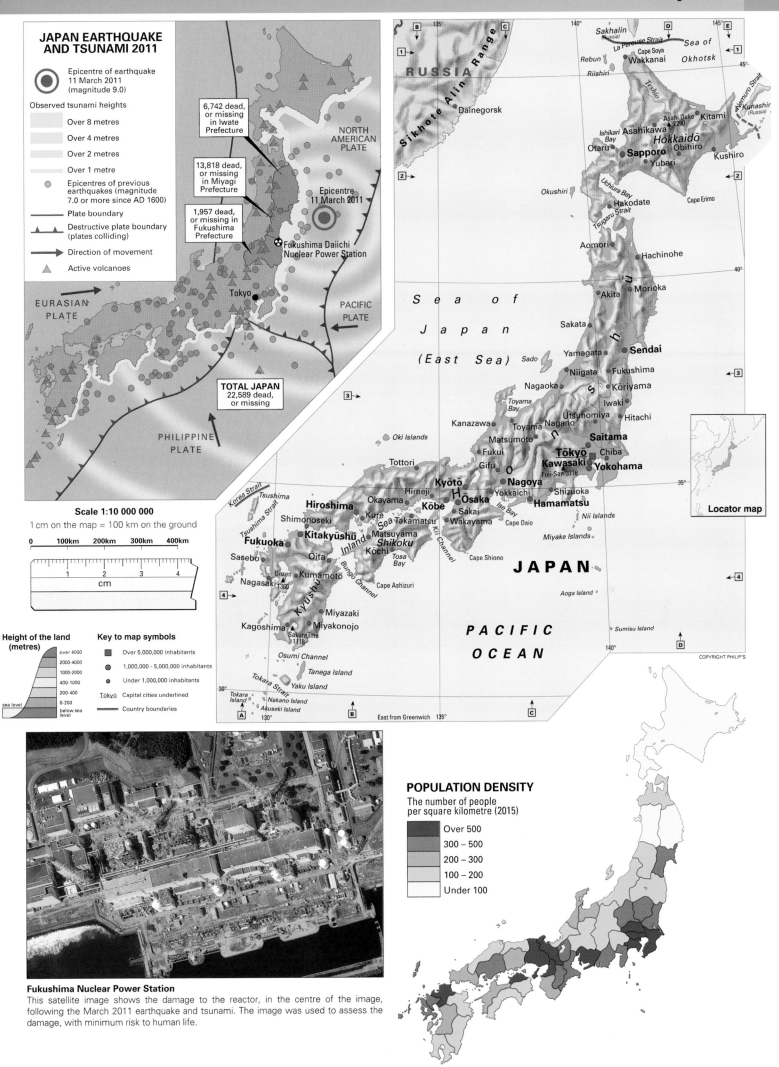

JAPAN EARTHQUAKE AND TSUNAMI 2011

Epicentre of earthquake 11 March 2011 (magnitude 9.0)

Observed tsunami heights
- Over 8 metres
- Over 4 metres
- Over 2 metres
- Over 1 metre

Epicentres of previous earthquakes (magnitude 7.0 or more since AD 1600)

Plate boundary

Destructive plate boundary (plates colliding)

Direction of movement

Active volcanoes

6,742 dead, or missing in Iwate Prefecture

13,818 dead, or missing in Miyagi Prefecture

1,957 dead, or missing in Fukushima Prefecture

Epicentre 11 March 2011

Fukushima Daiichi Nuclear Power Station

Tokyo

TOTAL JAPAN
22,589 dead, or missing

NORTH AMERICAN PLATE

EURASIAN PLATE

PACIFIC PLATE

PHILIPPINE PLATE

Scale 1:10 000 000

1 cm on the map = 100 km on the ground

0   100km   200km   300km   400km

cm

Height of the land (metres)
- over 4000
- 2000–4000
- 1000–2000
- 400–1000
- 200–400
- 0–200
- below sea level
- sea level

Key to map symbols
- Over 5,000,000 inhabitants
- 1,000,000 – 5,000,000 inhabitants
- Under 1,000,000 inhabitants
- Tōkyō Capital cities underlined
- Country boundaries

Locator map

COPYRIGHT PHILIP'S

Fukushima Nuclear Power Station
This satellite image shows the damage to the reactor, in the centre of the image, following the March 2011 earthquake and tsunami. The image was used to assess the damage, with minimum risk to human life.

POPULATION DENSITY
The number of people per square kilometre (2015)
- Over 500
- 300 – 500
- 200 – 300
- 100 – 200
- Under 100

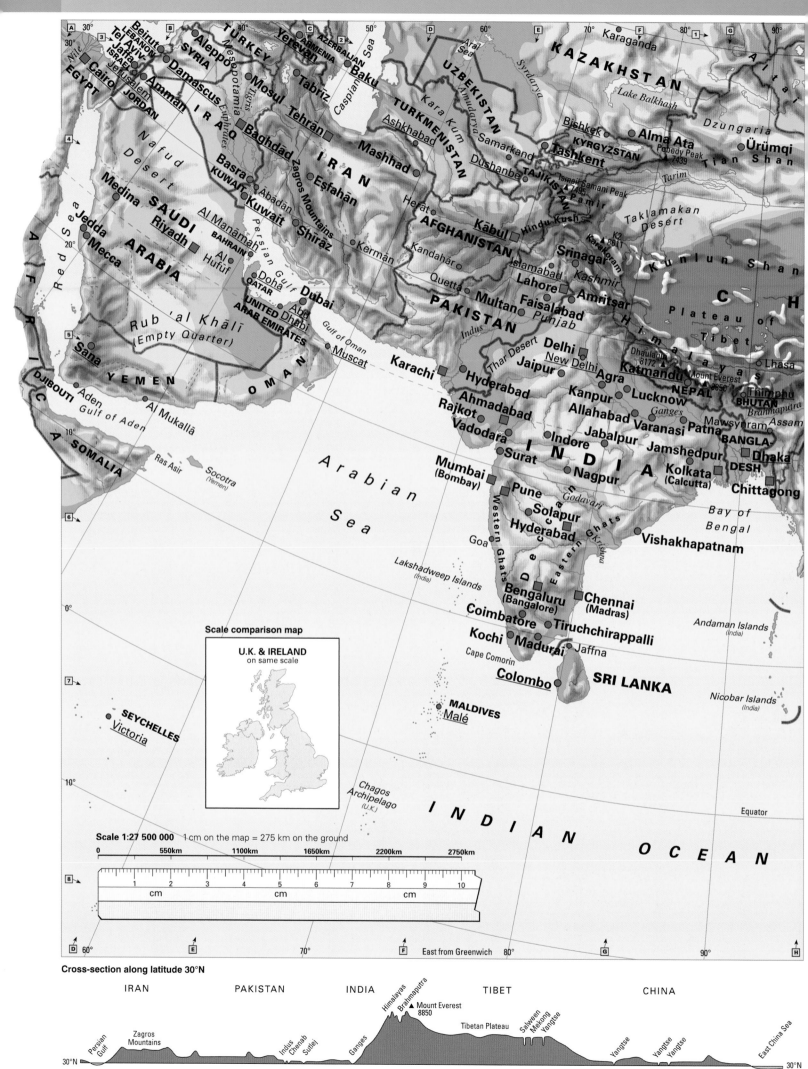

Cross-section along latitude 30°N

IRAN   PAKISTAN   INDIA   TIBET   CHINA

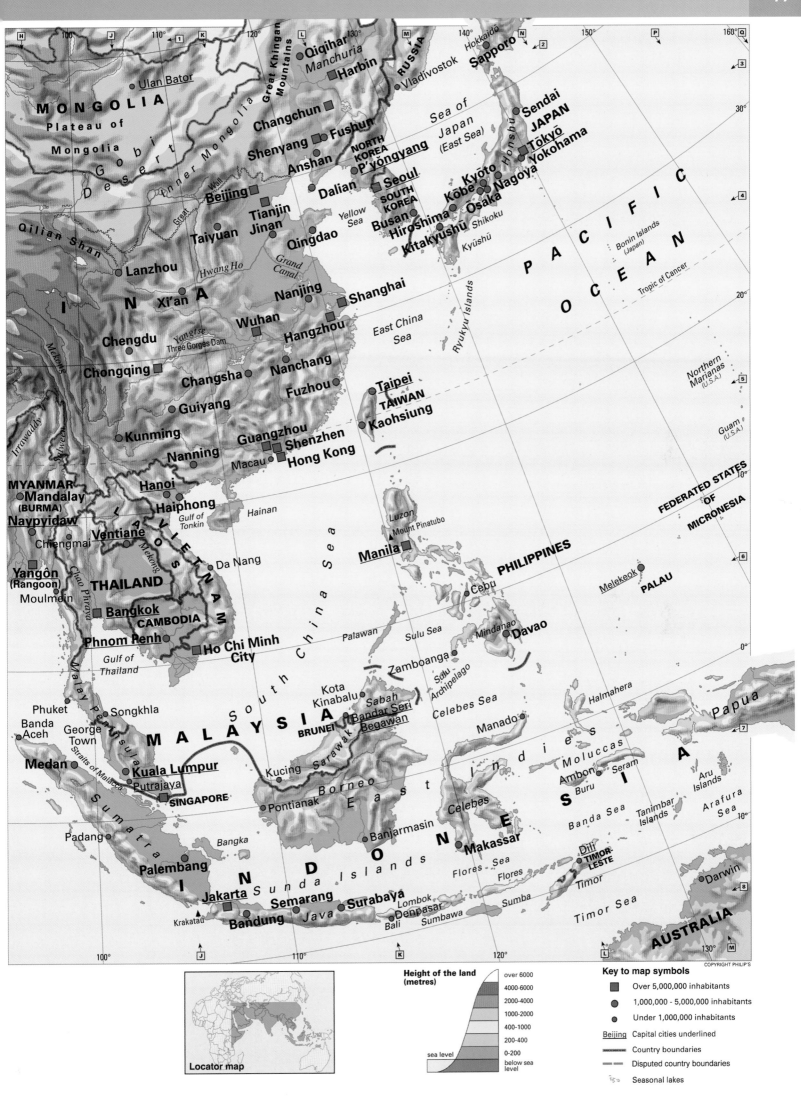

Height of the land
(metres)

over 6000	
4000-6000	
2000-4000	
1000-2000	
400-1000	
200-400	
0-200	
sea level	
below sea level	

Locator map

Key to map symbols

■ Over 5,000,000 inhabitants

● 1,000,000 - 5,000,000 inhabitants

• Under 1,000,000 inhabitants

<u>Beijing</u> Capital cities underlined

━━━ Country boundaries

─ ─ ─ Disputed country boundaries

Seasonal lakes

COPYRIGHT PHILIP'S

TURKMENISTAN

Kara Kum

Askhabad
Türkmenbashi
Bojnūrd
Neyshābūr
Mashhad
Birjand

Dasht-e Lūt

Dasht-e Kavir
(Great Salt Desert)

Kerman
Bam

I R A N

Caspian Sea

Bābol
Dāmāvand 5604
Karaj
Tehrān
Qom
Kāshān
Arāk
Yazd
Sirjān 4075
Bandar-e Abbās

Strait of Hormuz
Gulf of Oman

Suḥār
Muscat 3019

O M A N

East from Greenwich

COPYRIGHT PHILIP'S

Baku
AZERBAIJAN
Gäncä
NAGORNO-KARABAKH
NAXÇIVAN
(Azerbaijan)
Ardabil
Tabrīz
Lake Urmia
Zanjān
Qazvīn
Rasht
As Sulaymānīyah
Sanandaj
Hamadān
Kermānshāh
Esfahān

Zagros Mountains
4431
Khorramābād
Dezfūl
Ahvāz
Abādān

Shīrāz
Persepolis
Būshehr
Jahrom

Kharg Island
Persian Gulf

Ra's al Khaymah
Sharjah
Dubai
Al 'Ayn
Abu Dhabi

UNITED ARAB EMIRATES

GEORGIA Tbilisi
Batumi
ARMENIA
Yerevan
Mount Ararat 5165

Pontine Mountains
Trabzon
Erzurum
Van
Lake Van

Kurdistan

Mosul
Irbil
Kirkuk
Baghdād
Al Kūt
Tigris
Euphrates
Babylon
Al Hillah
An Najaf
An Nāşirīyah
Basra

KUWAIT
Kuwait

Al Jubayl
Ad Dammam
Dhahran
Al Mubarraz
Al Hufūf
Harad

BAHRAIN Al Manāmah
QATAR Doha

Black Sea

Samsun
Sivas
Ankara
Eskişehir
Kayseri
Malatya
Elâziğ
Diyarbakır
Şanlıurfa

Taurus Mountains

Konya
Afyon
İçel
Adana
Gaziantep
Aleppo
Latakia
Hamāh
SYRIA
Homs
Dayr az Zawr

Mesopotamia

Syrian Desert

Nafud Desert

Ḥā'il
Buraydah
Riyadh
As Sulaymānīyah

S A U D I   A R A B I A

Rub' al Khālī (Empty Quarter)

İstanbul
Bursa
Balıkesir
Manisa
İzmir
Denizli
Antalya

Anatolia

T U R K E Y

Troy

GREECE

Rhodes (Greece)

CYPRUS
Nicosia 1951

Mediterranean Sea

Tripoli
LEBANON
Beirut
Damascus
'Ammān
JORDAN
Jerusalem
WEST BANK
Amman
-422
Dead Sea
GAZA STRIP
Haifa
ISRAEL
Tel Aviv-Jaffa
Aqaba
Eilat

Tabūk

Medina
At Tā'if
Mecca

Tropic of Cancer

Yanbu 'al Bahr
Jedda

Red Sea

Port Said
Ismā'īlīya
Suez Canal
Suez
Alexandria
Cairo
Pyramids
Nile
Asyūt
Karnak
Thebes
Aswān
Lake Nasser
Sinai 2637
Sharm el Sheikh
Hurghada
Quseir

E G Y P T

Height of the land (metres)

over 6000
4000–6000
2000–4000
1000–2000
400–1000
200–400
0–200
below sea level
sea level

Key to map symbols

Over 5,000,000 inhabitants
1,000,000 – 5,000,000 inhabitants
Under 1,000,000 inhabitants
Baghdad Capital cities underlined
Country boundaries
Disputed country boundaries
Historical sites
Seasonal lakes
Seasonal rivers

Scale 1:12 000 000   1 cm on the map = 120 km on the ground

0   200km   400km   600km   800km

Locator map

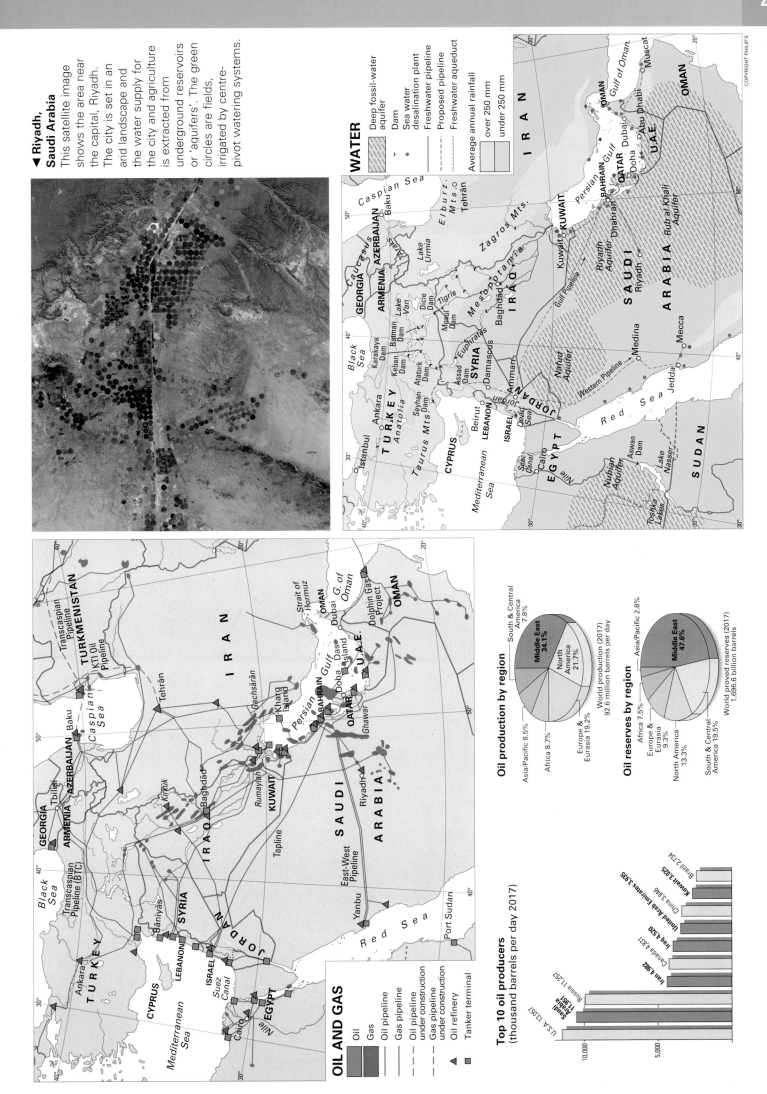

Riyadh, Saudi Arabia
This satellite image shows the area near the capital, Riyadh. The city is set in an arid landscape and the water supply for the city and agriculture is extracted from underground reservoirs or 'aquifers'. The green circles are fields, irrigated by centre-pivot watering systems.

WATER

Deep fossil-water aquifer
Dam
Sea water desalination plant
Freshwater pipeline
Proposed pipeline
Freshwater aqueduct
Average annual rainfall
over 250 mm
under 250 mm

OIL AND GAS

Oil
Gas
Oil pipeline
Gas pipeline
Oil pipeline under construction
Gas pipeline under construction
Oil refinery
Tanker terminal

Oil production by region
World production (2017) 92.6 million barrels per day
Middle East 34.1%
North America 21.7%
Europe & Eurasia 19.2%
Africa 8.7%
Asia/Pacific 8.5%
South & Central America 7.8%

Oil reserves by region
World proved reserves (2017) 1,696.6 billion barrels
Middle East 47.6%
South & Central America 19.5%
North America 13.3%
Europe & Eurasia 9.3%
Africa 7.5%
Asia/Pacific 2.8%

Top 10 oil producers (thousand barrels per day 2017)
U.S.A. 13,057
Saudi Arabia 11,951
Russia 11,257
Iran 4,982
Canada 4,831
Iraq 4,520
United Arab Emirates 3,935
China 3,846
Kuwait 3,025
Brazil 2,734

COPYRIGHT PHILIP'S

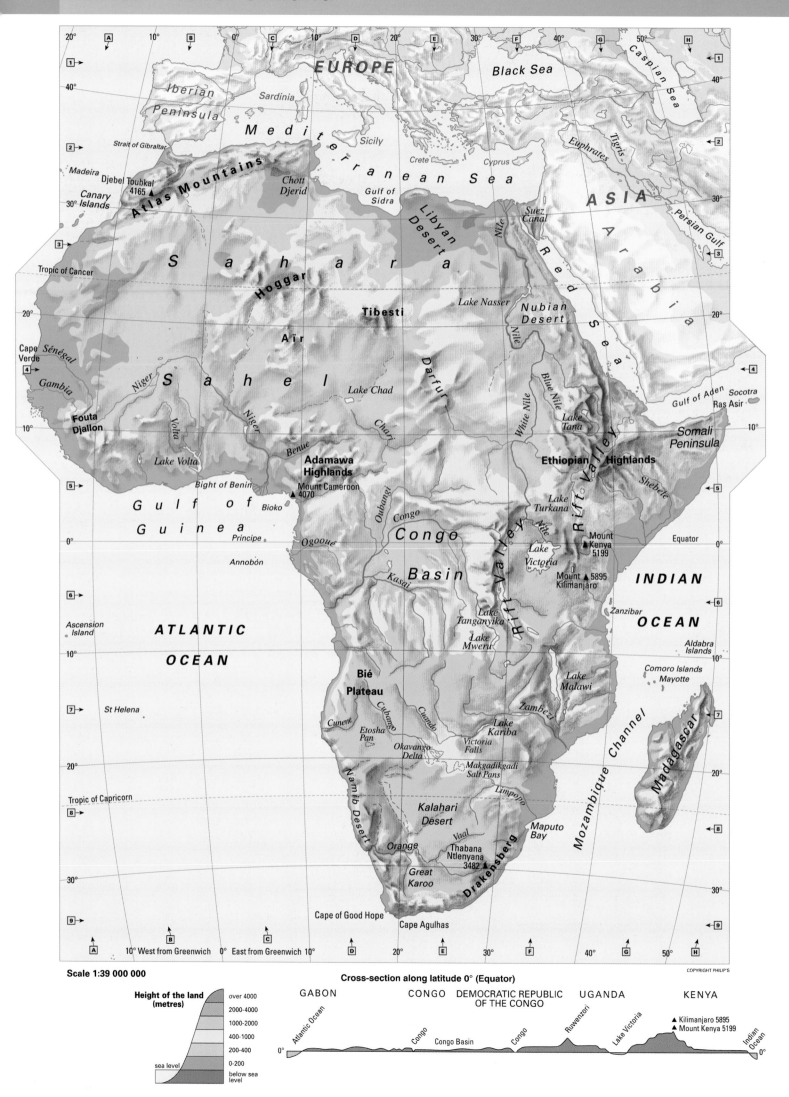

EUROPE

Iberian
Peninsula
Strait of Gibraltar
Madeira
Canary
Islands
Djebel Toubkal
4165
Atlas Mountains
Chott
Djerid
Sardinia
Sicily
Crete
Cyprus
M e d i t e r r a n e a n   S e a
Gulf of
Sidra

Black Sea
Caspian Sea
Euphrates
Tigris
A S I A
Suez Canal
Nile
Persian Gulf
Arabia
Red Sea

Cape
Verde
Sénégal
Gambia
Fouta
Djallon
Niger
S a h e l
Volta
Lake Volta
Niger
Benue
Adamawa
Highlands
Mount Cameroon
4070
Bioko
Principe
Annobón

S a h a r a
Hoggar
Aïr
Tibesti
Libyan
Desert
Darfur
Lake Chad
Chari
Bight of Benin
G u l f   o f
G u i n e a
Ogooué

Lake Nasser
Nubian
Desert
Nile
White Nile
Blue Nile
Lake
Tana
Ethiopian Highlands
Shebele
Lake
Turkana
Mount
Kenya
5199
Mount
Kilimanjaro
5895
Gulf of Aden
Somali
Peninsula
Socotra
Ras Asir
Rift Valley
Atile
Lake
Victoria

Tropic of Cancer

Oubangi
Congo
Kasai
C o n g o
B a s i n

Rift Valley

Equator
INDIAN
OCEAN
Zanzibar
Aldabra
Islands

A T L A N T I C
O C E A N
Ascension
Island
St Helena

Bié
Plateau
Cunene
Cubango
Etosha
Pan
Okavango
Delta
Namib Desert
Orange
Vaal
Great
Karoo
Cape of Good Hope
Cape Agulhas

Lake
Tanganyika
Lake
Mweru
Lake
Malawi
Comoro Islands
Mayotte
Zambezi
Lake
Kariba
Victoria
Falls
Cuando
Makgadikgadi
Salt Pans
Kalahari
Desert
Limpopo
Thabana
Ntlenyana
3482
Drakensberg
Maputo
Bay
Mozambique Channel
Madagascar

Tropic of Capricorn

Height of the land
(metres)

over 4000
2000-4000
1000-2000
400-1000
200-400
0-200
sea level
below sea
level

Cross-section along latitude 0° (Equator)

GABON   CONGO   DEMOCRATIC REPUBLIC   UGANDA   KENYA
OF THE CONGO

Atlantic Ocean
Congo
Congo Basin
Congo
Ruwenzori
Lake Victoria
Indian Ocean

▲ Kilimanjaro 5895
▲ Mount Kenya 5199

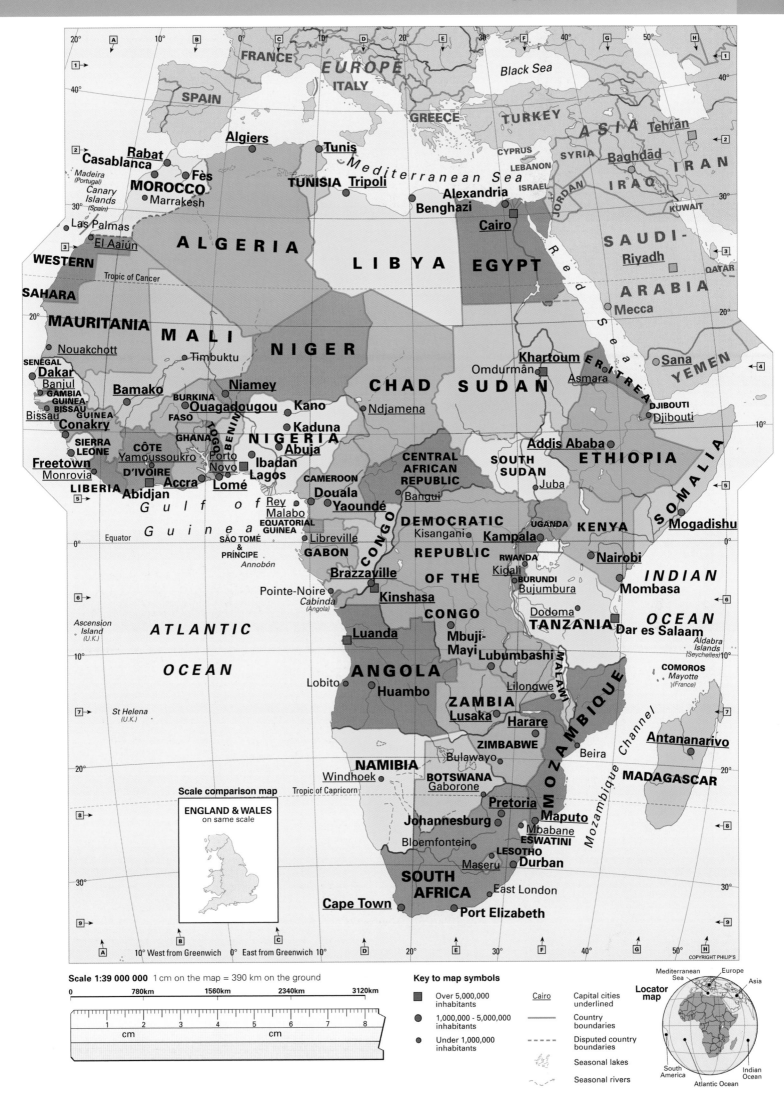

Scale comparison map

ENGLAND & WALES
on same scale

Scale 1:39 000 000   1 cm on the map = 390 km on the ground

0   780km   1560km   2340km   3120km

cm   cm

Key to map symbols

Over 5,000,000 inhabitants

1,000,000 – 5,000,000 inhabitants

Under 1,000,000 inhabitants

Cairo — Capital cities underlined

—— Country boundaries

----- Disputed country boundaries

Seasonal lakes

Seasonal rivers

Locator map

COPYRIGHT PHILIP'S

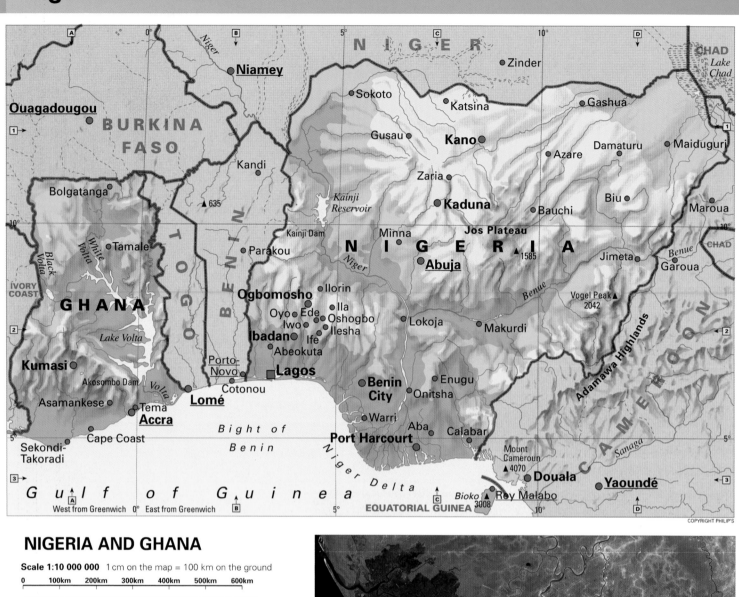

COPYRIGHT PHILIP'S

NIGERIA AND GHANA

Scale 1:10 000 000   1 cm on the map = 100 km on the ground

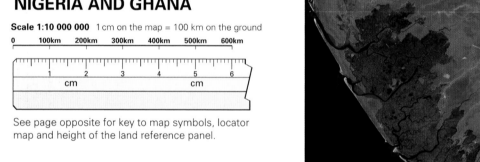

0   100km   200km   300km   400km   500km   600km

1   2   3   4   5   6
cm   cm

See page opposite for key to map symbols, locator
map and height of the land reference panel.

Niger Delta, Nigeria ▲

Satellite imagery helps to plan the drilling for oil
and gas in the delta and to monitor the effect of
the drilling on this fragile environment. This is a
false colour image which shows vegetation such
as mangrove swamps in dark red.

OIL AND GAS IN THE NIGER DELTA

Oilfields	Gas pipelines
Oil pipelines	Tanker terminals
Gasfields	Oil refineries

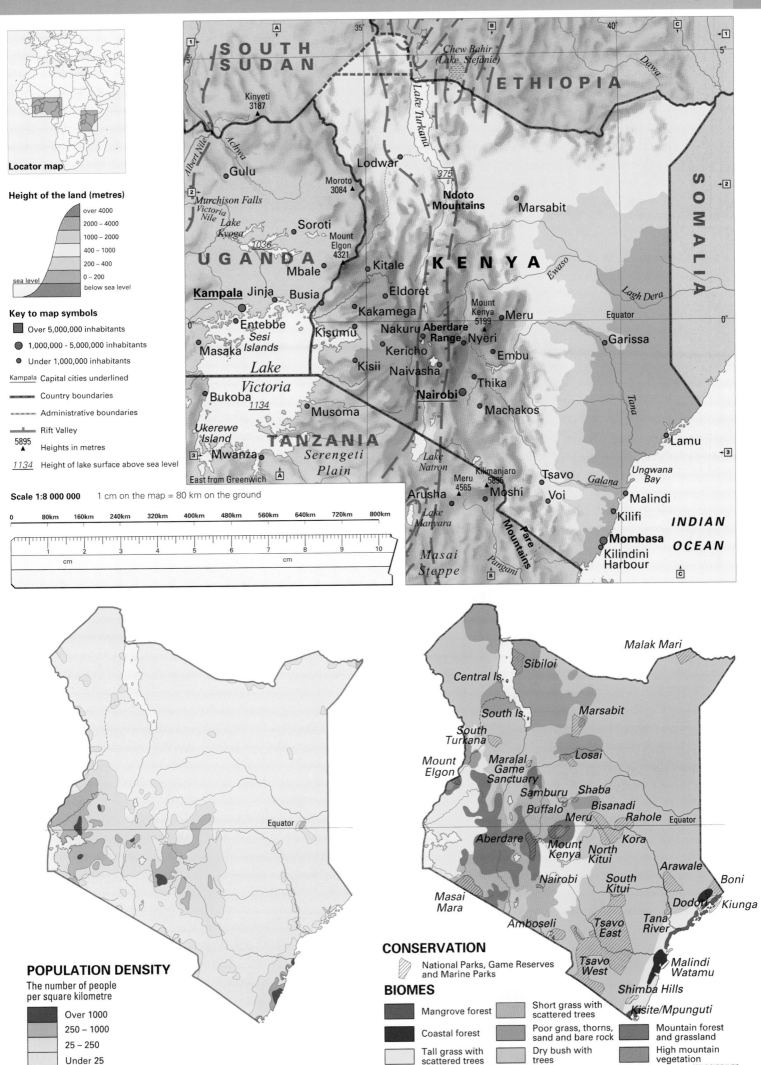

Locator map

Height of the land (metres)

- over 4000
- 2000 – 4000
- 1000 – 2000
- 400 – 1000
- 200 – 400
- 0 – 200
- sea level
- below sea level

Key to map symbols

- Over 5,000,000 inhabitants
- 1,000,000 - 5,000,000 inhabitants
- Under 1,000,000 inhabitants
- Kampala Capital cities underlined
- Country boundaries
- Administrative boundaries
- Rift Valley
- 5895 ▲ Heights in metres
- 1134 Height of lake surface above sea level

Scale 1:8 000 000
1 cm on the map = 80 km on the ground

0 80km 160km 240km 320km 400km 480km 560km 640km 720km 800km

cm   cm

East from Greenwich

Map labels

SOUTH SUDAN

Kinyeti 3187

Gulu

Murchison Falls
Victoria Nile
Lake Kyoga

UGANDA

Soroti

Mount Elgon 4321

Mbale

Kampala Jinja Busia

Entebbe
Sesi Islands

Masaka

Bukoba

Lake Victoria 1134

Ukerewe Island

Mwanza

Musoma

TANZANIA

Serengeti Plain

Masai Steppe

Lake Manyara

Arusha

Lodwar

Moroto 3084 ▲

Lake Turkana

375

Ndoto Mountains

Marsabit

ETHIOPIA

Chew Bahir (Lake Stefanie)

Dawa

SOMALIA

Lagh Dera

KENYA

Kitale

Eldoret

Kakamega

Kisumu

Kisii

Kericho

Nakuru Aberdare Range Nyeri

Naivasha

Meru

Mount Kenya 5199

Ewaso

Equator

Garissa

Embu

Thika

Nairobi

Machakos

Lake Natron

Kilimanjaro 5895 ▲

Meru 4565 ▲ Moshi

Voi

Tsavo

Galana

Tana

Lamu

Ungwana Bay

Malindi

Kilifi

INDIAN OCEAN

Mombasa
Kilindini Harbour

Pare Mountains

Pangani

POPULATION DENSITY

The number of people per square kilometre

- Over 1000
- 250 – 1000
- 25 – 250
- Under 25

Equator

CONSERVATION

National Parks, Game Reserves and Marine Parks

BIOMES

- Mangrove forest
- Coastal forest
- Tall grass with scattered trees
- Short grass with scattered trees
- Poor grass, thorns, sand and bare rock
- Dry bush with trees
- Mountain forest and grassland
- High mountain vegetation

Malak Mari

Central Is. Sibiloi

South Is.

South Turkana

Mount Elgon

Marsabit

Maralal Game Sanctuary

Losai

Samburu Shaba

Buffalo Bisanadi Rahole

Meru

Aberdare

Mount Kenya

North Kitui

Kora

Arawale

Boni

Nairobi

South Kitui

Dodori Kiunga

Masai Mara

Amboseli

Tsavo East

Tana River

Malindi Watamu

Tsavo West

Shimba Hills

Kisite/Mpunguti

COPYRIGHT PHILIP'S

Cross-section along longitude 147°E A U S T R A L I A
North   South
147°E   Great Barrier Reef   Great Divide   Darling   Murray   Mount Kosciuszko 2228 ▲ Snowy Mountains   Bass Strait   Tasmania   147°E

Height of the land (metres)
- over 4000
- 2000-4000
- 1000-2000
- 400-1000
- 200-400
- 0-200
- sea level
- below sea level

Key to map symbols

- Over 5,000,000 inhabitants
- 1,000,000 - 5,000,000 inhabitants
- Under 1,000,000 inhabitants
- Canberra Capital cities underlined

- Country boundaries
- State boundaries
- Seasonal lakes
- Seasonal rivers

Locator map
Asia
Pacific Ocean
Indian Ocean
Southern Ocean
Antarctica

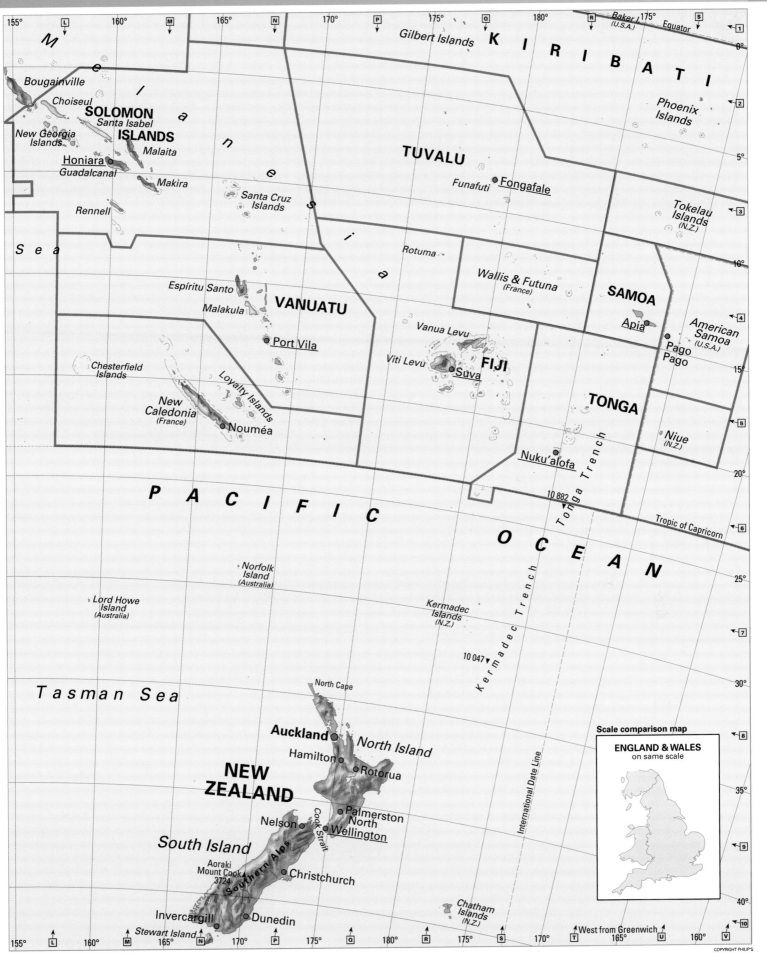

M

L↓ 155° M↓ 160° 165° N↓ 170° P 175° Q 180° R Baker I. 175° S Equator 1→
(U.S.A.)

0°

Gilbert Islands K I R I B A T I

M
e
l
a
n
e
s
i
a

Bougainville

Choiseul

SOLOMON
Santa Isabel

ISLANDS
New Georgia
Islands

Malaita

Honiara
Guadalcanal

Makira

Rennell

Santa Cruz
Islands

Phoenix
Islands

2→

3→

TUVALU

5°

Funafuti Fongafale

Tokelau
Islands
(N.Z.)

Sea

S e a

Rotuma

10°

Espíritu Santo

Malakula

VANUATU

Port Vila

Wallis & Futuna
(France)

SAMOA

Apia

American
Samoa
(U.S.A.)

Pago
Pago

4→

15°

Chesterfield
Islands

New
Caledonia
(France)

Loyalty Islands

Nouméa

Vanua Levu

Viti Levu

Suva

FIJI

TONGA

Niue
(N.Z.)

5

Nuku'alofa

20°

10 882

Tonga Trench

Tropic of Capricorn

6→

P A C I F I C

O C E A N

Norfolk
Island
(Australia)

25°

Lord Howe
Island
(Australia)

Kermadec
Islands
(N.Z.)

Kermadec Trench

7

10 047▼

30°

T a s m a n   S e a

North Cape

Auckland

Hamilton

Rotorua

North Island

8→

NEW
ZEALAND

International Date Line

ENGLAND & WALES
on same scale

35°

Palmerston
North

Nelson

Cook Strait

Wellington

South Island

Aoraki
Mount Cook
3724

Southern Alps

Christchurch

9→

Invercargill

Dunedin

Stewart Island

Chatham
Islands
(N.Z.)

40°

West from Greenwich

10→

L 155° M 160° 165° N 170° P 175° Q 180° R 175° S 170° T 165° U 160° V

COPYRIGHT PHILIP'S

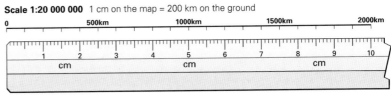

Scale 1:20 000 000   1 cm on the map = 200 km on the ground

0   500km   1000km   1500km   2000km

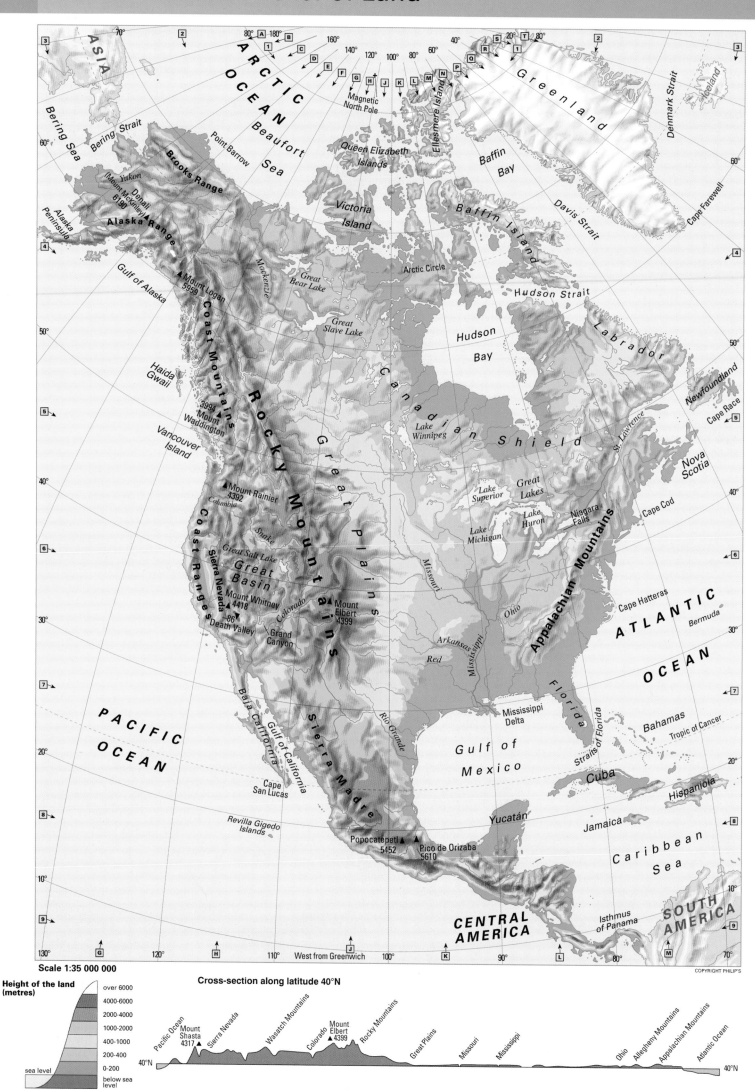

ASIA

ARCTIC OCEAN

Bering Sea
Bering Strait
Point Barrow
Beaufort Sea
Brooks Range
Alaska Peninsula
Yukon
Denali (Mount McKinley)▲ 6190
Alaska Range
Gulf of Alaska
▲ Mount Logan 5959
Mackenzie
Great Bear Lake
Victoria Island
Queen Elizabeth Islands
Magnetic North Pole
Ellesmere Island
Baffin Bay
Baffin Island
Greenland
Denmark Strait
Iceland
Davis Strait
Cape Farewell

Haida Gwaii
Coast Mountains
▲ 3994 Mount Waddington
Vancouver Island
Rocky Mountains
Great Plains
Arctic Circle
Great Slave Lake
Hudson Bay
Hudson Strait
Labrador
Canadian Shield
Lake Winnipeg
St. Lawrence
Newfoundland
Cape Race
Nova Scotia

Columbia
▲ Mount Rainier 4392
Snake
Great Salt Lake
Great Basin
Sierra Nevada
▲ Mount Whitney 4418
Death Valley -86
Grand Canyon
Colorado
Coast Ranges
Lake Superior
Lake Michigan
Lake Huron
Great Lakes
Niagara Falls
Appalachian Mountains
Cape Cod
Cape Hatteras
Bermuda
ATLANTIC OCEAN

▲ Mount Elbert 4399
Missouri
Arkansas
Red
Mississippi
Ohio
Florida

PACIFIC OCEAN
Baja California
Gulf of California
Cape San Lucas
Revilla Gigedo Islands
Sierra Madre
Rio Grande
Gulf of Mexico
Mississippi Delta
Straits of Florida
Bahamas
Tropic of Cancer
Cuba
Jamaica
Hispaniola
Caribbean Sea

Popocatépetl ▲ 5452
Pico de Orizaba ▲ 5610
Yucatán

CENTRAL AMERICA
Isthmus of Panama
SOUTH AMERICA

West from Greenwich

Scale 1:35 000 000

COPYRIGHT PHILIP'S

Height of the land (metres)

over 6000
4000-6000
2000-4000
1000-2000
400-1000
200-400
0-200
below sea level
sea level

Cross-section along latitude 40°N

40°N
Pacific Ocean
Mount Shasta 4317
Sierra Nevada
Wasatch Mountains
Colorado
Mount Elbert ▲ 4399
Rocky Mountains
Great Plains
Missouri
Mississippi
Ohio
Allegheny Mountains
Appalachian Mountains
Atlantic Ocean
40°N

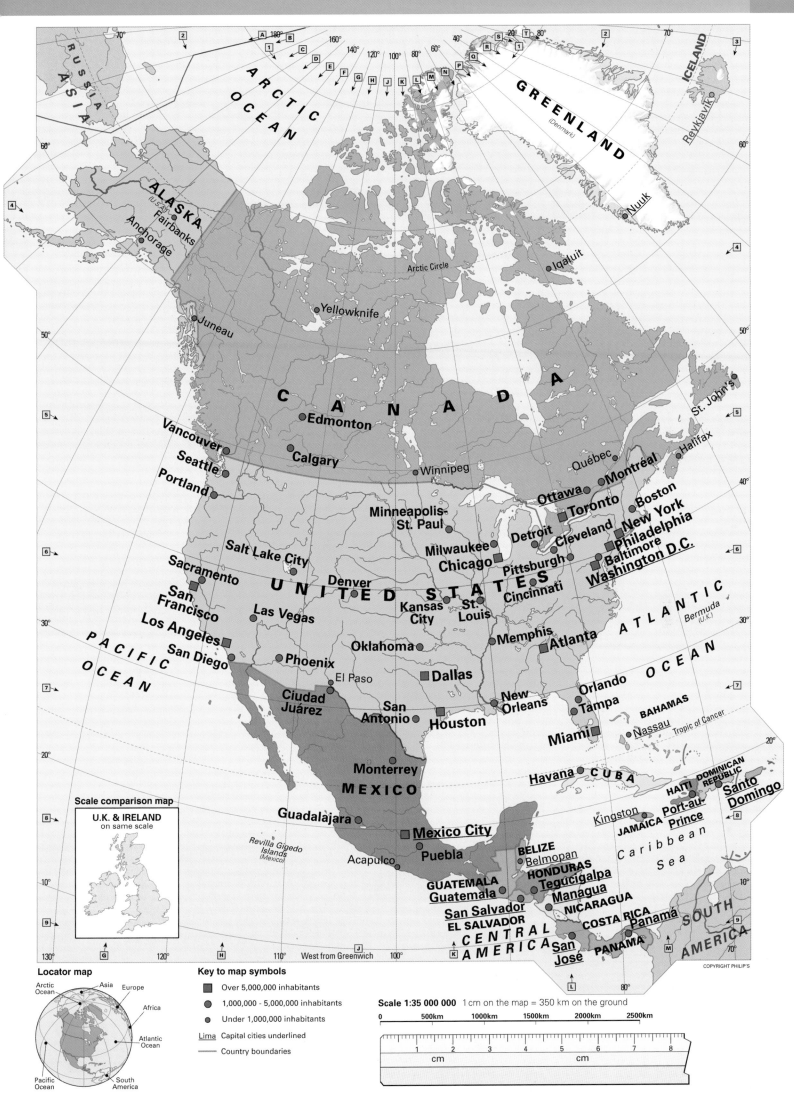

ASIA
RUSSIA

ARCTIC OCEAN

GREENLAND
(Denmark)

ICELAND
Reykjavik

ALASKA
(U.S.A.)
Fairbanks
Anchorage

Nuuk

Juneau

Arctic Circle

Iqaluit

Yellowknife

C A N A D A

Edmonton

St. John's

Vancouver
Seattle
Portland

Calgary

Winnipeg

Québec
Ottawa
Montréal
Toronto
Detroit
Cleveland

Halifax
Boston
New York
Philadelphia
Baltimore
Washington D.C.

Minneapolis-
St. Paul

Milwaukee
Chicago

Salt Lake City

Sacramento

San
Francisco

Denver

U N I T E D   S T A T E S

Pittsburgh
Cincinnati

ATLANTIC

Bermuda
(U.K.)

Las Vegas

Kansas
City

St.
Louis

Los Angeles
San Diego

Phoenix

Oklahoma

Memphis

Atlanta

OCEAN

PACIFIC
OCEAN

El Paso

Ciudad
Juárez

San
Antonio

Dallas

New
Orleans

Houston

Orlando
Tampa

BAHAMAS

Miami

Nassau

Tropic of Cancer

Monterrey

Havana   CUBA

HAITI   DOMINICAN
REPUBLIC

M E X I C O

Santo
Domingo

Scale comparison map

U.K. & IRELAND
on same scale

Guadalajara

Mexico City

Kingston
JAMAICA

Port-au-
Prince

Caribbean
Sea

Revilla Gigedo
Islands
(Mexico)

Acapulco

Puebla

BELIZE
Belmopan

HONDURAS

GUATEMALA
Guatemala

Tegucigalpa
Managua

NICARAGUA

San Salvador
EL SALVADOR

COSTA RICA

Panamá

SOUTH

C E N T R A L
A M E R I C A

San
José

PANAMA

AMERICA

COPYRIGHT PHILIP'S

Locator map

Arctic
Ocean

Asia   Europe

Africa

Atlantic
Ocean

Pacific
Ocean

South
America

Key to map symbols

■ Over 5,000,000 inhabitants

● 1,000,000 - 5,000,000 inhabitants

• Under 1,000,000 inhabitants

Lima Capital cities underlined

—— Country boundaries

Scale 1:35 000 000   1 cm on the map = 350 km on the ground

0   500km   1000km   1500km   2000km   2500km

1   2   3   4   5   6   7   8
cm   cm

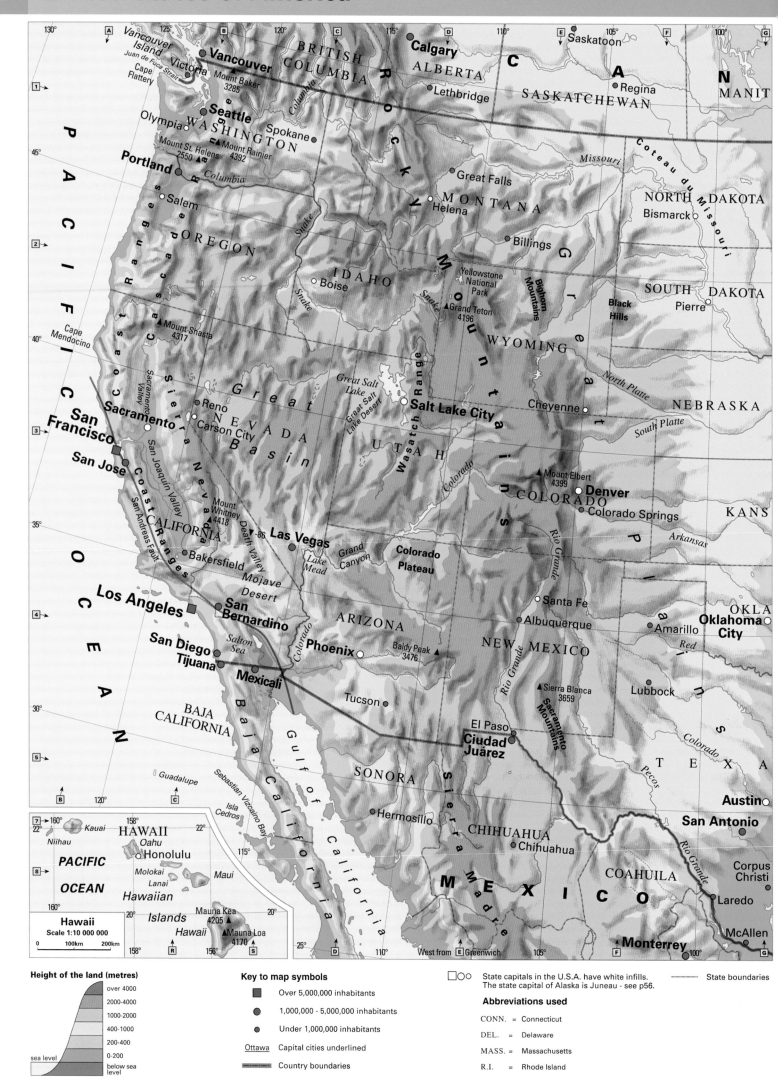

Height of the land (metres)

over 4000
2000-4000
1000-2000
400-1000
200-400
0-200

sea level

below sea level

Key to map symbols

◼ Over 5,000,000 inhabitants

● 1,000,000 - 5,000,000 inhabitants

• Under 1,000,000 inhabitants

<u>Ottawa</u> Capital cities underlined

Country boundaries

☐○○ State capitals in the U.S.A. have white infills.
The state capital of Alaska is Juneau - see p56.

——— State boundaries

Abbreviations used

CONN. = Connecticut

DEL. = Delaware

MASS. = Massachusetts

R.I. = Rhode Island

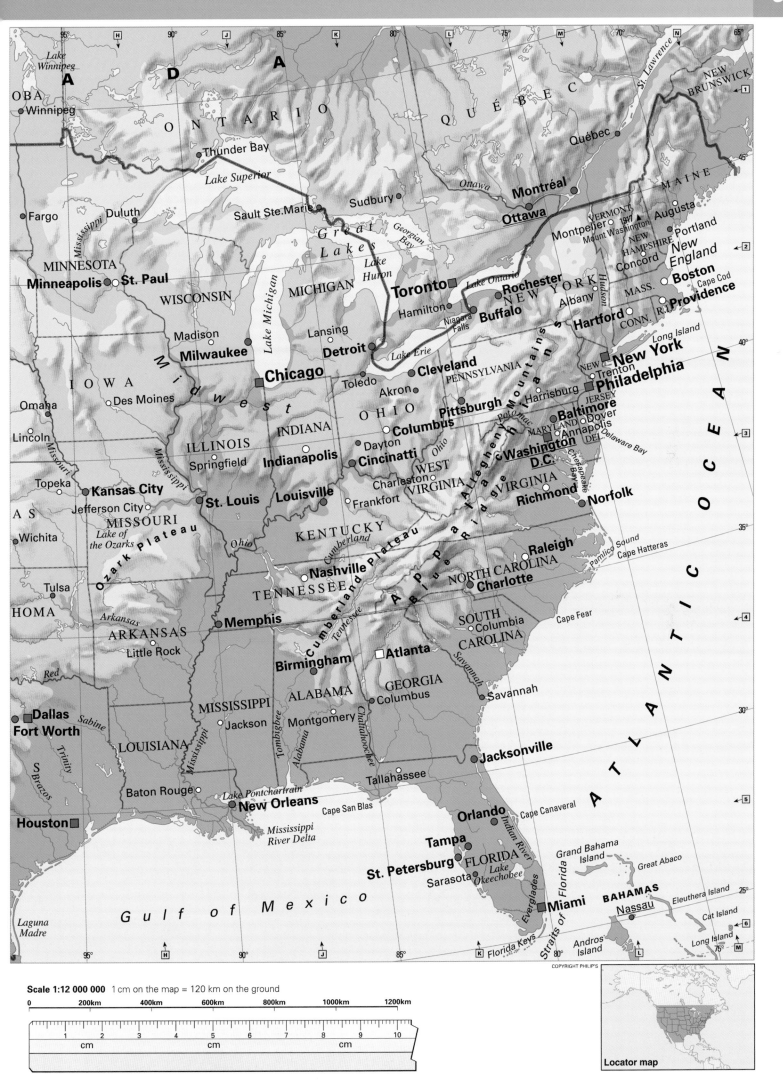

Scale 1:12 000 000   1 cm on the map = 120 km on the ground

0   200km   400km   600km   800km   1000km   1200km

COPYRIGHT PHILIP'S

Locator map

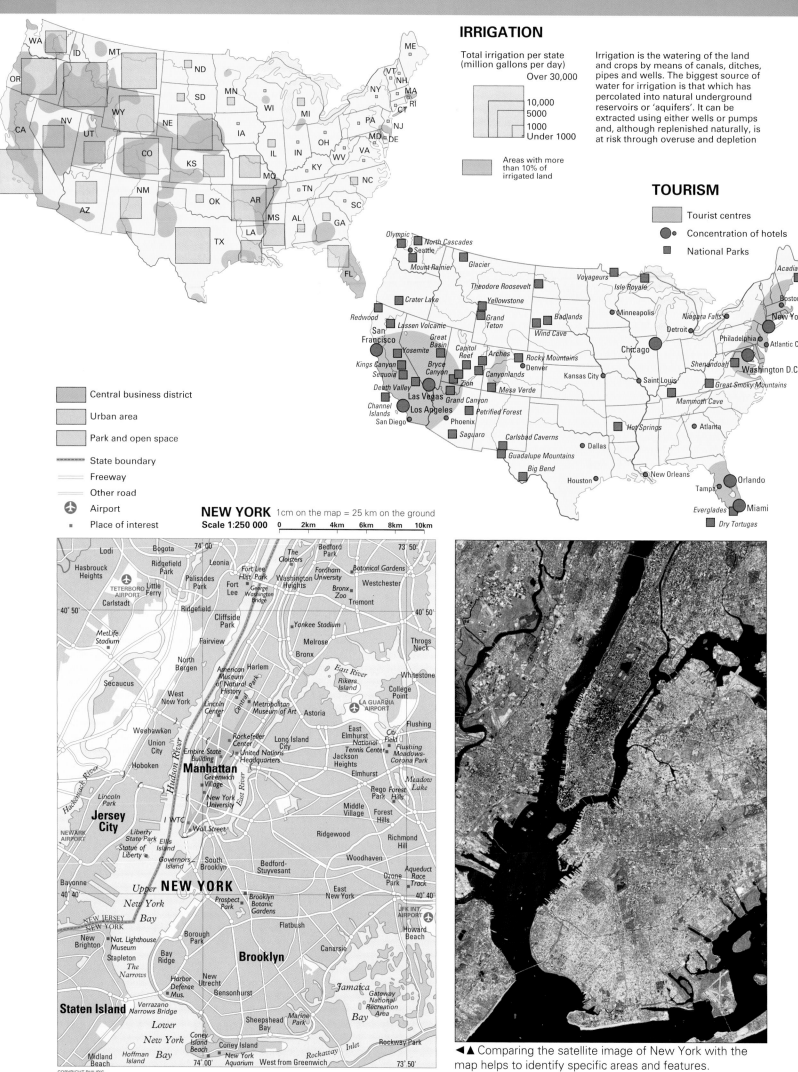

IRRIGATION

Total irrigation per state
(million gallons per day)

Over 30,000

10,000
5000
1000
Under 1000

Areas with more
than 10% of
irrigated land

Irrigation is the watering of the land
and crops by means of canals, ditches,
pipes and wells. The biggest source of
water for irrigation is that which has
percolated into natural underground
reservoirs or 'aquifers'. It can be
extracted using either wells or pumps
and, although replenished naturally, is
at risk through overuse and depletion

Map state labels: WA, ID, MT, OR, ND, ME, VT, NH, MA, NY, RI, CT, NV, WY, MN, SD, WI, MI, PA, NJ, CA, UT, NE, IA, OH, IN, MD, DE, CO, KS, IL, WV, VA, NM, MO, KY, NC, AZ, OK, AR, TN, SC, TX, MS, AL, GA, LA, FL

TOURISM

Tourist centres

Concentration of hotels

National Parks

Tourism map labels: Olympic, North Cascades, Seattle, Mount Rainier, Glacier, Theodore Roosevelt, Voyageurs, Isle Royale, Acadia, Crater Lake, Yellowstone, Badlands, Minneapolis, Niagara Falls, Boston, Redwood, Lassen Volcanic, Grand Teton, Wind Cave, Detroit, New Yo..., San Francisco, Great Basin, Capitol Reef, Arches, Rocky Mountains, Chicago, Philadelphia, Atlantic C..., Yosemite, Bryce Canyon, Canyonlands, Denver, Kings Canyon, Sequoia, Zion, Mesa Verde, Kansas City, Saint Louis, Shenandoah, Washington D.C, Death Valley, Las Vegas, Grand Canyon, Great Smoky Mountains, Channel Islands, Los Angeles, Petrified Forest, Phoenix, Mammoth Cave, San Diego, Saguaro, Carlsbad Caverns, Hot Springs, Atlanta, Dallas, Guadalupe Mountains, Big Bend, Houston, New Orleans, Orlando, Tampa, Everglades, Miami, Dry Tortugas

Legend

- Central business district
- Urban area
- Park and open space
- State boundary
- Freeway
- Other road
- ✈ Airport
- ▪ Place of interest

NEW YORK

1cm on the map = 25 km on the ground

Scale 1:250 000

0   2km   4km   6km   8km   10km

New York map labels: Lodi, Bogota, Ridgefield Park, Leonia, The Cloisters, Bedford Park, Botanical Gardens, Hasbrouck Heights, Fort Lee Hist. Park, Washington Heights, Fordham University, Westchester, TETERBORO AIRPORT, Little Ferry, Palisades Park, Fort Lee, George Washington Bridge, Bronx Zoo, Tremont, Carlstadt, Ridgefield, Cliffside Park, Yankee Stadium, MetLife Stadium, Fairview, Melrose, Throgs Neck, North Bergen, American Museum of Natural History, Harlem, Bronx, Whitestone, Secaucus, West New York, Central Park, East River, Rikers Island, College Point, Weehawken, Lincoln Center, Metropolitan Museum of Art, Astoria, LA GUARDIA AIRPORT, Union City, Rockefeller Center, Long Island City, East Elmhurst, Citi Field, Flushing, Hoboken, Empire State Building, United Nations Headquarters, National Tennis Center, Flushing Meadows-Corona Park, Jackson Heights, Elmhurst, Meadow Lake, Manhattan, Greenwich Village, New York University, Rego Park, Forest Hills, Lincoln Park, I WTC, Wall Street, Middle Village, Forest Hills, Jersey City, Liberty State Park, Ellis Island, Statue of Liberty, Governors Island, South Brooklyn, Bedford-Stuyvesant, Ridgewood, Woodhaven, Richmond Hill, Bayonne, NEWARK AIRPORT, Upper New York Bay, NEW YORK, Prospect Park, Brooklyn Botanic Gardens, Flatbush, East New York, Ozone Park, Aqueduct Race Track, Howard Beach, JFK INT. AIRPORT, New Jersey/New York, New Brighton, Nat. Lighthouse Museum, Stapleton, The Narrows, Borough Park, Bay Ridge, New Utrecht, Bensonhurst, Canarsie, Brooklyn, Staten Island, Harbor Defense Mus., Gateway National Recreation Area, Lower New York Bay, Sheepshead Bay, Marine Park, Jamaica Bay, Verrazano Narrows Bridge, Coney Island Beach, Coney Island, New York Aquarium, Midland Beach, Hoffman Island, West from Greenwich, Rockaway Park, Inlet

COPYRIGHT PHILIP'S

◀▲ Comparing the satellite image of New York with the
map helps to identify specific areas and features.

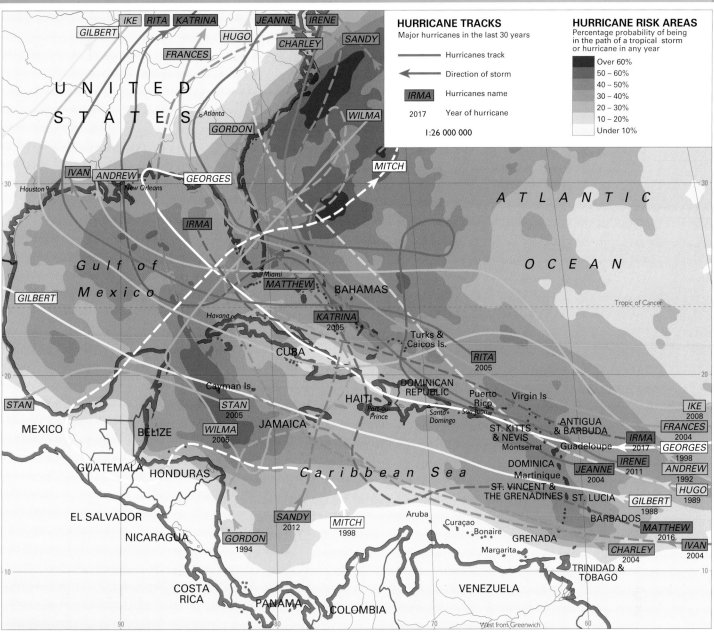

HURRICANE TRACKS
Major hurricanes in the last 30 years

→ Hurricanes track

← Direction of storm

IRMA   Hurricanes name

2017   Year of hurricane

1:26 000 000

HURRICANE RISK AREAS
Percentage probability of being
in the path of a tropical storm
or hurricane in any year

- Over 60%
- 50 – 60%
- 40 – 50%
- 30 – 40%
- 20 – 30%
- 10 – 20%
- Under 10%

▲ **Hurricane Irma,** with winds of 295km per hour, was the
most powerful in over ten years when it made landfall on
Barbuda in September 2017. It caused catastrophic damage
in St. Barthélemy, St. Martin, Anguilla and the Virgin Islands.

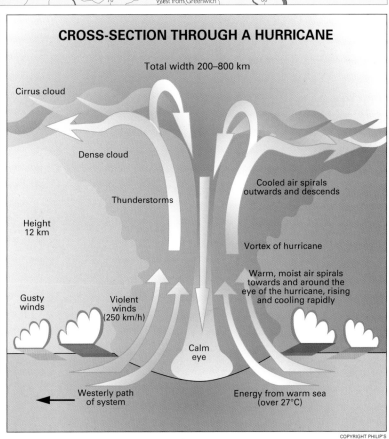

CROSS-SECTION THROUGH A HURRICANE

Total width 200–800 km

Cirrus cloud

Dense cloud

Thunderstorms

Cooled air spirals
outwards and descends

Height
12 km

Vortex of hurricane

Warm, moist air spirals
towards and around the
eye of the hurricane, rising
and cooling rapidly

Gusty
winds

Violent
winds
(250 km/h)

Calm
eye

Westerly path
of system

Energy from warm sea
(over 27°C)

Tijuana
Mexicali
Bataques
Phoenix
Tucson
El Paso
Nogales
Ciudad Juárez
Río Grande do Norte
UNITED STATE
Dallas
Birmingham
Austin
Houston
San Antonio
New Orleans
Hermosillo
Chihuahua
Nuevo Laredo
Corpus Christi
Mississippi River Delta
Ciudad Obregón
3050
Los Mochis
Torreón
Reynosa
Gulf of Mexico
La Paz
Culiacán
Monterrey
Matamoros
Cabo San Lucas
Durango
MEXICO
Mazatlán
Tropic of Cancer
San Luis Potosí
Tampico
Las Tres Marias
Aguascalientes
León
Guadalajara
Cabo Corrientes
Querétaro
Mérida
Cancún
Revilla Gigedo Islands
Volcán Popocatepetl
5610
Gulf of Campeche
Cozumel
Mexico
5452
Pico de Orizaba
Cuernavaca
Puebla
Veracruz
Campeche
Yucatán
Balsas
Villahermosa
Acapulco
Oaxaca
Isthmus of Tehuantepec
Belize City
Belmopan
BELIZE
Tuxtla Gutiérrez
Gulf of Honduras
GUATEMALA
Puerto Barrios
Gulf of Tehuantepec
4093
San Pedro Sula
Guatemala
HONDURAS
San Salvador
Tegucigalp
EL SALVADOR
NICARAG
Managua
Lake Nicaragua

P A C I F I C

O C E A N

Scale comparison map

ENGLAND & WALES
on same scale

Height of the land (metres)

over 4000	
2000-4000	
1000-2000	
400-1000	
200-400	
0-200	
sea level	
below sea level	

Key to map symbols

▪ Over 5,000,000 inhabitants

● 1,000,000 - 5,000,000 inhabitants

• Under 1,000,000 inhabitants

Mexico Capital cities underlined

——— Country boundaries

West from Greenwich

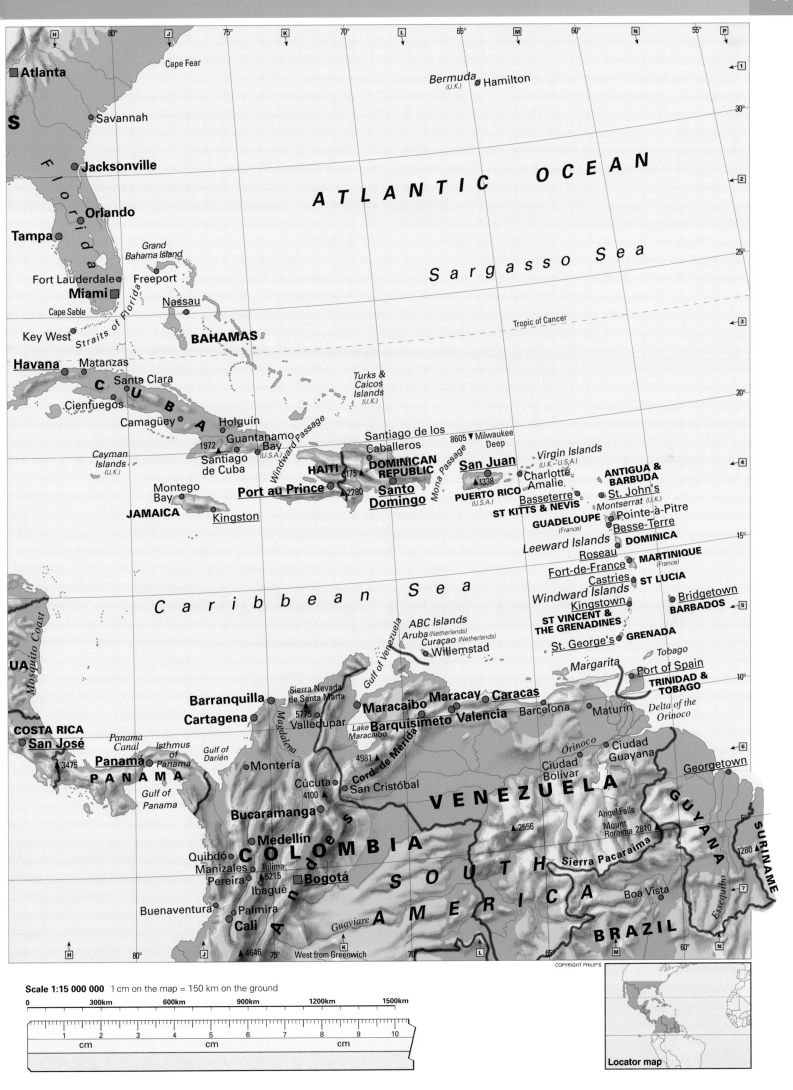

Atlanta

Savannah

Jacksonville

Florida

Orlando

Tampa

Fort Lauderdale

Miami

Cape Sable

Key West

Havana Matanzas

Santa Clara

Cienfuegos

CUBA

Camagüey

Holguín

1972

Guantanamo Bay (U.S.A.)

Santiago de Cuba

Cayman Islands (U.K.)

Montego Bay

JAMAICA Kingston

Cape Fear

Grand Bahama Island

Freeport

Nassau

BAHAMAS

Turks & Caicos Islands (U.K.)

Windward Passage

Santiago de los Caballeros

DOMINICAN REPUBLIC

3175

HAITI

Port au Prince

2280

Santo Domingo

Mona Passage

8605 ▼ Milwaukee Deep

San Juan

1338

PUERTO RICO (U.S.A.)

Virgin Islands (U.K.–U.S.A.)

Charlotte Amalie

Basseterre

ST KITTS & NEVIS

ANTIGUA & BARBUDA

St. John's

Montserrat (U.K.)

GUADELOUPE (France)

Pointe-à-Pitre

Basse-Terre

Leeward Islands

DOMINICA

Roseau

MARTINIQUE (France)

Fort-de-France

Castries ST LUCIA

Windward Islands

Kingstown

ST VINCENT & THE GRENADINES

Bridgetown

BARBADOS

St. George's GRENADA

ATLANTIC OCEAN

Sargasso Sea

Tropic of Cancer

Bermuda (U.K.) Hamilton

Caribbean Sea

Tobago

Margarita

Port of Spain

TRINIDAD & TOBAGO

ABC Islands

Aruba (Netherlands)

Curaçao (Netherlands)

Willemstad

Gulf of Venezuela

Barranquilla

Cartagena

Sierra Nevada de Santa Marta

5775

Valledupar

Maracaibo

Lake Maracaibo

Barquisimeto

Maracay

Valencia

Caracas

Barcelona

Maturín

Delta of the Orinoco

MOSQUITO COAST

UA

COSTA RICA

San José

3475

Panamá

PANAMA

Panama Canal

Isthmus of Panama

Gulf of Darién

Gulf of Panama

Montería

Cúcuta

4981

4100

San Cristóbal

Cord. de Mérida

Bucaramanga

Medellín

Quibdó

Manizales

Tolima

Pereira

5215

Ibagué

Bogotá

Buenaventura

Palmira

Cali

4646

Magdalena

Andes

COLOMBIA

VENEZUELA

Orinoco

Ciudad Bolívar

Ciudad Guayana

Georgetown

GUYANA

SURINAME

1280

2556

Angel Falls

Mount Roraima 2810

Sierra Pacaraima

Boa Vista

SOUTH AMERICA

BRAZIL

Guaviare

Esequibo

West from Greenwich

COPYRIGHT PHILIP'S

Scale 1:15 000 000 1 cm on the map = 150 km on the ground

0   300km   600km   900km   1200km   1500km

1   2   3   4   5   6   7   8   9   10

cm   cm   cm

Locator map

Cross-section along latitude 20°S

CHILE   BOLIVIA   PARAGUAY   BRAZIL

▲ Ojos del Salado 6863
▲ Ancohuma & Illampu 6550

Height of the land (metres)

- over 4000
- 3000 – 4000
- 2000 – 3000
- 1000 – 2000
- 500 – 1000
- 200 – 500
- 0 – 200
- below sea level

Scale 1:35 000 000

COPYRIGHT PHILIP'S

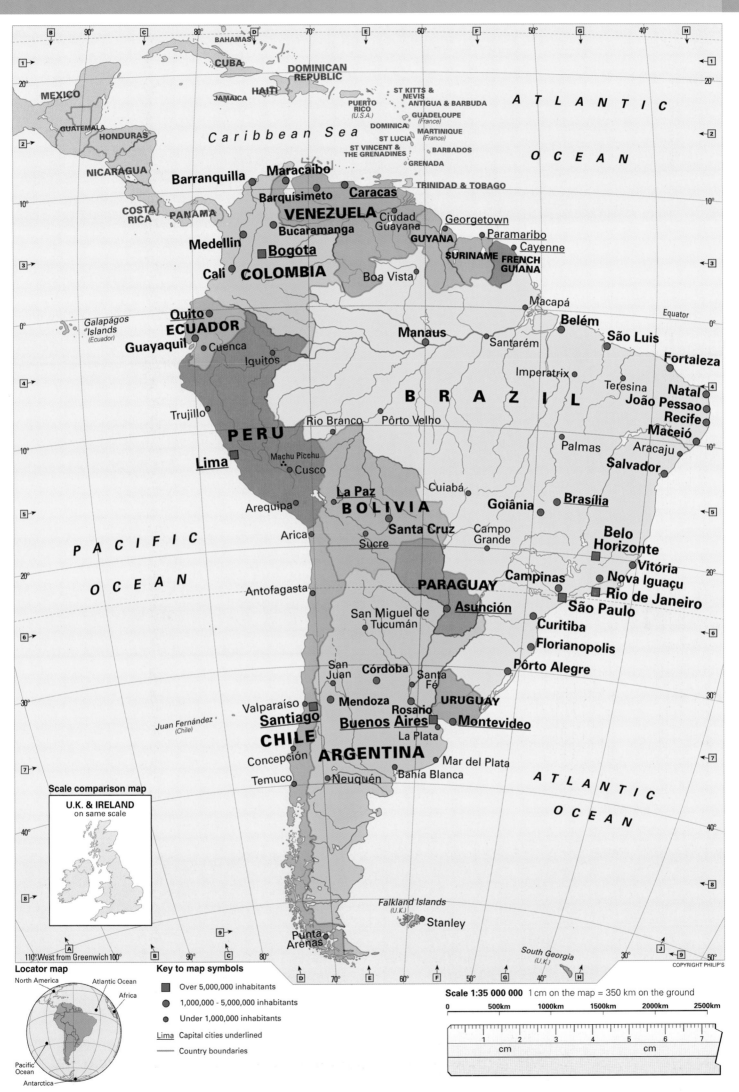

Scale comparison map

U.K. & IRELAND
on same scale

Locator map

Key to map symbols

■ Over 5,000,000 inhabitants

● 1,000,000 – 5,000,000 inhabitants

• Under 1,000,000 inhabitants

<u>Lima</u> Capital cities underlined

— Country boundaries

Scale 1:35 000 000 1 cm on the map = 350 km on the ground

0   500km   1000km   1500km   2000km   2500km

COPYRIGHT PHILIP'S

Locator map

ATLANTIC OCEAN

VENEZUELA
SURINAME
FRENCH GUIANA
GUYANA
COLOMBIA
Orinoco
Boa Vista
Pico de Neblina 2994 ▲
Guiana Highlands
RORAIMA
Uaupés
Negro
Branco
AMAPÁ
Macapá
Equator
Bragança
Belém
São Luís
Parnaíba
Japurá
Solimões
Içá
Putumayo
Manaus
Santarém
Amazon
Fortaleza
Tapajós
PARÁ
Bacabal
MARANHÃO
Teresina
Mossoró
RIO GRANDE DO NORTE
A M A Z O N A S
Juruá
Purus
Madeira
Marabá
Imperatriz
CEARÁ
Natal
João Pessoa
Juàzeiro do Norte
PARAÍBA
Campina Grande
Recife
Selvas
Aripuanã
Telês Pires
Xingu
Araguaia
Tocantins
PIAUÍ
PERNAMBUCO
ACRE
Pôrto Velho
B R A Z I L
Sobradinho Reservoir
São Francisco
Juàzeiro
Maceió
ALAGOAS
Rio Branco
RONDÔNIA
Palmas
TOCANTINS
B A H Í A
Aracaju
SERGIPE
PERU
Mamoré
Guaporé
MATO GROSSO
Feira de Santana
Salvador
BOLIVIA
Paraguay
Cuiabá
Vitória da Conquista
Itabuna
Anápolis
Brasília
Montes Claros
Teófilo Otoni
ESPÍRITO SANTO
Goiânia
GOIÁS
MATO GROSSO DO SUL
Uberlândia
MINAS GERAIS
Pico da Bandeira 2890 ▲
Vitória
Campo Grande
SÃO PAULO
Ribeirão Prêto
Juiz de Fora
Campos
Araçatuba
Bauru
Nova Iguaçu
Paraná
Londrina
Campinas
Rio de Janeiro
Tropic of Capricorn
PARAGUAY
PARANÁ
São Paulo
Santos
Ponta Grossa
Foz do Iguaçu
Curitiba
Iguaçu
ARGENTINA
SANTA CATARINA
Joinville
Florianópolis
ATLANTIC OCEAN
Caxias do Sul
RIO GRANDE DO SUL
Pôrto Alegre
Uruguaiana
Lagoa dos Patos
Pelotas
URUGUAY
West from Greenwich

Scale 1:21 000 000   1 cm on the map = 210 km on the ground

| 0 | 210km | 420km | 630km | 840km | 1050km | 1260km |

cm

Height of the land (metres)

over 4000
2000 – 4000
1000 – 2000
400 – 1000
200 – 400
0 – 200
sea level
below sea level

Key to map symbols

■ Over 5,000,000 inhabitants
● 1,000,000 – 5,000,000 inhabitants
• Under 1,000,000 inhabitants
Brasília Capital cities underlined
Country boundaries
State boundaries

WEALTH
The value of total production divided by the population in US$ (2016)

Over $10,000
$7,500 – 10,000
$5,000 – 7,500
Under $5,000

COPYRIGHT PHILIP'S

POPULATION DENSITY
The number of people per square kilometre (2017)

Over 100
50 – 100
10 – 50
Under 10

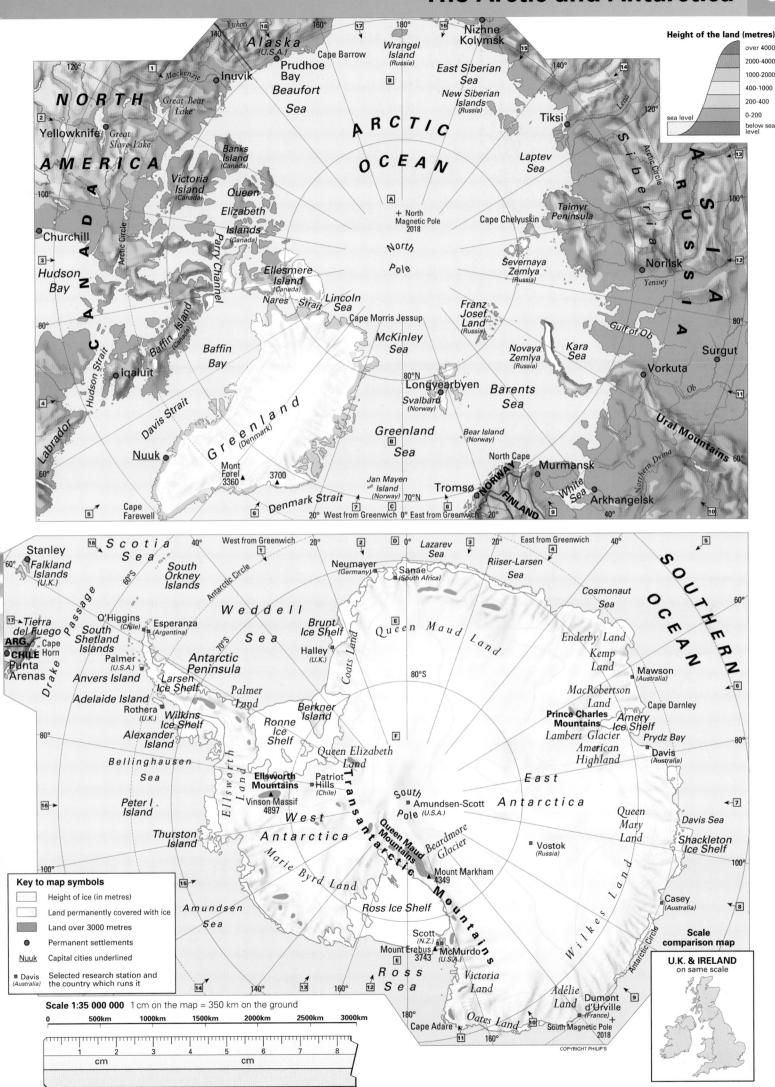

CONTINENT	AREA '000 kilometres	COLDEST PLACE degrees Celsius		HOTTEST PLACE degrees Celsius		WETTEST PLACE average annual rainfall, mm		DRIEST PLACE average annual rainfall, mm	
Asia	44,500	Oymyakon, Russia –70°C	①	Tirat Zevi, Israel 54°C	⑧	Mawsynram, India 11,870	⑮	Aden, Yemen 46	㉑
Africa	30,302	Ifrane, Morocco –24°C	②	Kebili, Tunisia 55°C	⑨	Debundscha, Cameroon 10,290	⑯	Wadi Haifa, Sudan 2	㉒
North America	24,241	Snag, Yukon –63°C	③	Death Valley, California 57°C	⑩	Henderson Lake, Canada 6,500	⑰	Bataques, Mexico 30	㉓
South America	17,793	Sarmiento, Argentina –33°C	④	Rivadavia, Argentina 49°C	⑪	Quibdó, Colombia 8,990	⑱	Quillagua, Chile 0.6	㉔
Antarctica	14,000	Vostok –89°C	⑤	Vanda Station 15°C	⑫				
Europe	9,957	Ust Shchugor, Russia –55°C	⑥	Seville, Spain 50°C	⑬	Crkvice, Montenegro 4,650	⑲	Astrakhan, Russia 160	㉕
Oceania	8,557	Charlotte Pass, Australia –22°C	⑦	Oodnadatta, Australia 51°C	⑭	Tully, Australia 4,550	⑳	Mulka, Australia 100	㉖

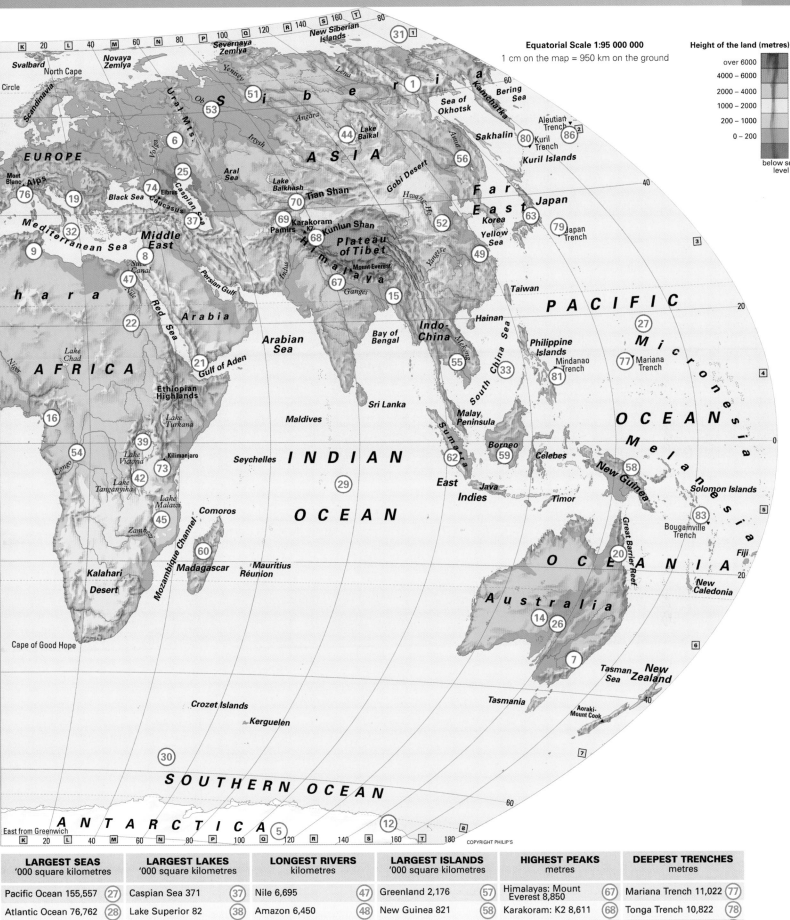

Equatorial Scale 1:95 000 000
1 cm on the map = 950 km on the ground

Height of the land (metres)

over 6000
4000 – 6000
2000 – 4000
1000 – 2000
200 – 1000
0 – 200

below sea level

COPYRIGHT PHILIP'S

LARGEST SEAS '000 square kilometres		LARGEST LAKES '000 square kilometres		LONGEST RIVERS kilometres		LARGEST ISLANDS '000 square kilometres		HIGHEST PEAKS metres		DEEPEST TRENCHES metres	
Pacific Ocean 155,557	27	Caspian Sea 371	37	Nile 6,695	47	Greenland 2,176	57	Himalayas: Mount Everest 8,850	67	Mariana Trench 11,022	77
Atlantic Ocean 76,762	28	Lake Superior 82	38	Amazon 6,450	48	New Guinea 821	58	Karakoram: K2 8,611	68	Tonga Trench 10,822	78
Indian Ocean 68,556	29	Lake Victoria 68	39	Yangtse 6,380	49	Borneo 744	59	Pamirs: Ismail Samani Peak 7,495	69	Japan Trench 10,554	79
Southern Ocean 20,237	30	Lake Huron 60	40	Mississippi-Missouri 5,971	50	Madagascar 587	60	Tian Shan: Pobedy Peak 7,439	70	Kuril Trench 10,542	80
Arctic Ocean 14,351	31	Lake Michigan 58	41	Yenisey-Angara 5,550	51	Baffin Island 508	61	Andes: Aconcagua 6,962	71	Mindanao Trench 10,497	81
Mediterranean Sea 2,966	32	Lake Tanganyika 33	42	Hwang-Ho 5,464	52	Sumatra 474	62	Rocky Mountains: Denali 6,190	72	Kermadec Trench 10,047	82
South China Sea 2,318	33	Great Bear Lake 32	43	Ob-Irtysh 5,410	53	Honshu 231	63	East Africa: Kilimanjaro 5,895	73	Bougainville Trench 9,140	83
Bering Sea 2,274	34	Lake Baikal 31	44	Congo 4,670	54	Great Britain 230	64	Caucasus: Elbrus 5,642	74	Milwaukee Deep 8,605	84
Caribbean Sea 1,942	35	Lake Malawi 30	45	Mekong 4,500	55	Victoria Island 212	65	Antarctica: Vinson Massif 4,897	75	South Sandwich Trench 7,235	85
Gulf of Mexico 1,813	36	Great Slave Lake 29	46	Amur 4,442	56	Ellesmere Island 197	66	Alps: Mont Blanc 4,808	76	Aleutian Trench 7,822	86

ALB. = ALBANIA
B.-H. = BOSNIA-HERZEGOVINA
BELG. = BELGIUM
CR. = CROATIA
CZECH. = CZECHIA
EST. = ESTONIA
HUNG. = HUNGARY
K. = KOSOVO
LAT. = LATVIA
LEB. = LEBANON
LITH. = LITHUANIA
LUX. = LUXEMBOURG

COUNTRY	'000 people	COUNTRY	'000 people	COUNTRY	'000 people	COUNTRY	'000 people	COUNTRY	'000 people
China	1,384,689	Mexico	125,959	France	67,364	Argentina	44,694	Saudi Arabia	33,091
India	1,296,834	Ethiopia	108,386	United Kingdom	65,105	Ukraine	43,952	Malaysia	31,810
USA	329,256	Philippines	105,893	Italy	62,247	Sudan	43,121	Venezuela	31,689
Indonesia	262,787	Egypt	99,413	Myanmar	55,623	Algeria	41,657	Peru	31,331
Brazil	208,847	Vietnam	97,040	Tanzania	55,451	Uganda	40,854	Angola	30,356
Pakistan	207,863	Congo (Dem. Rep.)	85,281	South Africa	54,842	Iraq	40,194	Uzbekistan	30,024
Nigeria	203,453	Iran	83,025	South Korea	51,418	Poland	38,421	Nepal	29,718
Bangladesh	159,453	Turkey	81,257	Spain	48,958	Canada	35,882	Yemen	28,667
Russia	142,123	Germany	80,458	Kenya	48,398	Afghanistan	34,941	Ghana	28,102
Japan	126,168	Thailand	68,616	Colombia	48,169	Morocco	34,314	Mozambique	27,234

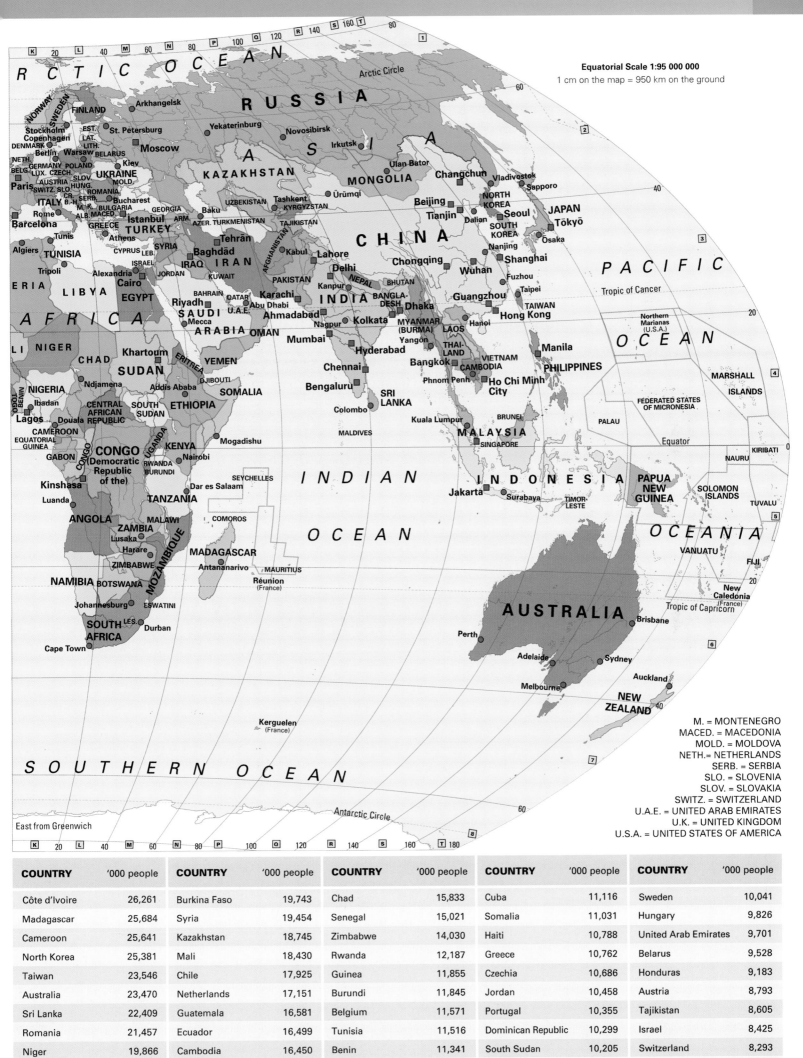

Equatorial Scale 1:95 000 000
1 cm on the map = 950 km on the ground

M. = MONTENEGRO
MACED. = MACEDONIA
MOLD. = MOLDOVA
NETH.= NETHERLANDS
SERB. = SERBIA
SLO. = SLOVENIA
SLOV. = SLOVAKIA
SWITZ. = SWITZERLAND
U.A.E. = UNITED ARAB EMIRATES
U.K. = UNITED KINGDOM
U.S.A. = UNITED STATES OF AMERICA

East from Greenwich

COUNTRY	'000 people	COUNTRY	'000 people	COUNTRY	'000 people	COUNTRY	'000 people	COUNTRY	'000 people
Côte d'Ivoire	26,261	Burkina Faso	19,743	Chad	15,833	Cuba	11,116	Sweden	10,041
Madagascar	25,684	Syria	19,454	Senegal	15,021	Somalia	11,031	Hungary	9,826
Cameroon	25,641	Kazakhstan	18,745	Zimbabwe	14,030	Haiti	10,788	United Arab Emirates	9,701
North Korea	25,381	Mali	18,430	Rwanda	12,187	Greece	10,762	Belarus	9,528
Taiwan	23,546	Chile	17,925	Guinea	11,855	Czechia	10,686	Honduras	9,183
Australia	23,470	Netherlands	17,151	Burundi	11,845	Jordan	10,458	Austria	8,793
Sri Lanka	22,409	Guatemala	16,581	Belgium	11,571	Portugal	10,355	Tajikistan	8,605
Romania	21,457	Ecuador	16,499	Tunisia	11,516	Dominican Republic	10,299	Israel	8,425
Niger	19,866	Cambodia	16,450	Benin	11,341	South Sudan	10,205	Switzerland	8,293
Malawi	19,843	Zambia	16,445	Bolivia	11,306	Azerbaijan	10,047	Togo	8,176

CLIMATE REGIONS

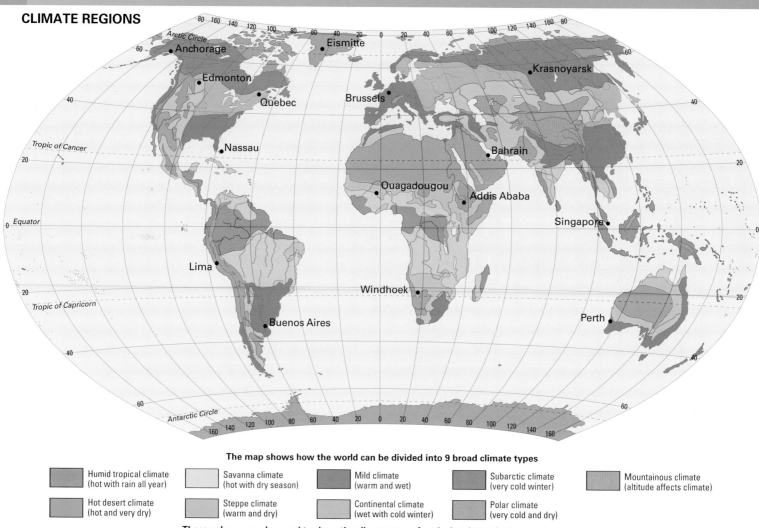

The map shows how the world can be divided into 9 broad climate types

Humid tropical climate (hot with rain all year)

Savanna climate (hot with dry season)

Mild climate (warm and wet)

Subarctic climate (very cold winter)

Mountainous climate (altitude affects climate)

Hot desert climate (hot and very dry)

Steppe climate (warm and dry)

Continental climate (wet with cold winter)

Polar climate (very cold and dry)

These colours are also used to show the climate type of each city shown in the graphs below

CLIMATE GRAPHS

The graphs below give examples of places within each climate region, showing how temperature and rainfall vary from month to month.

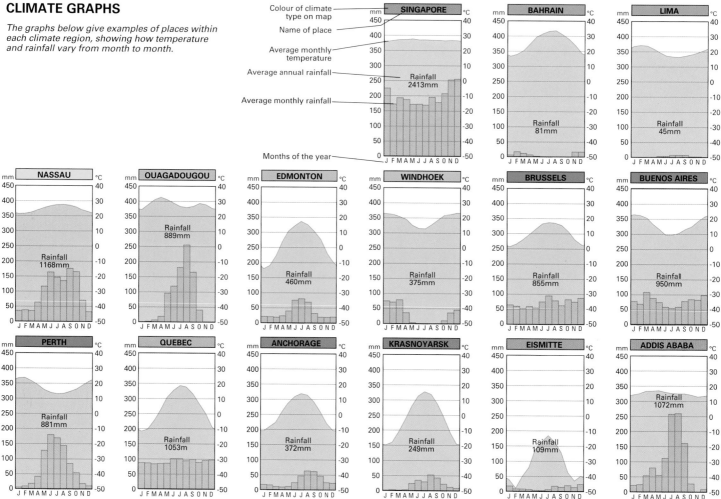

HUMID TROPICAL CLIMATE

HOT DESERT CLIMATE

SAVANNA CLIMATE

MILD CLIMATE

POLAR CLIMATE

MOUNTAINOUS CLIMATE

ANNUAL RAINFALL

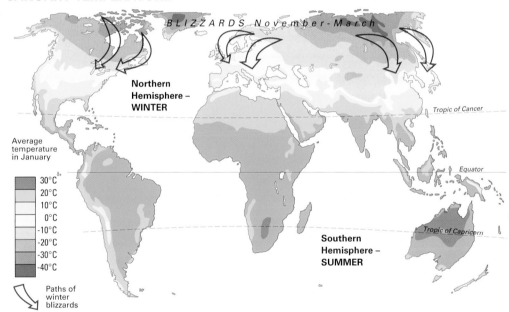

Tropic of Cancer

Equator

Tropic of Capricorn

Mawsynram, India
Over 11,800 mm
has fallen in a year
Wettest place
on Earth

Average annual
rainfall

3000 mm
2000 mm
1000 mm
500 mm
250 mm

Atacama Desert
Driest place on Earth
No rain has ever
been recorded

JANUARY TEMPERATURE

BLIZZARDS November-March

Northern
Hemisphere –
WINTER

Tropic of Cancer

Average
temperature
in January

30°C
20°C
10°C
0°C
-10°C
-20°C
-30°C
-40°C

Equator

Tropic of Capricorn

Southern
Hemisphere –
SUMMER

Paths of
winter
blizzards

JULY TEMPERATURE

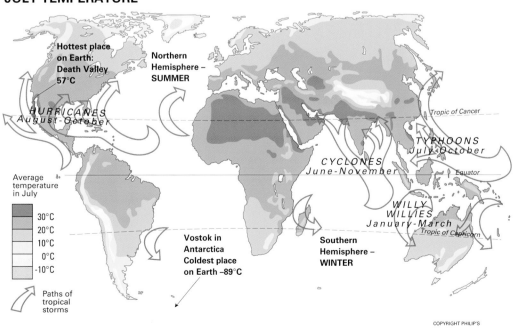

Hottest place
on Earth:
Death Valley
57°C

Northern
Hemisphere –
SUMMER

*HURRICANES
August-October*

Tropic of Cancer

*TYPHOONS
July-October*

*CYCLONES
June-November*

Equator

Average
temperature
in July

30°C
20°C
10°C
0°C
-10°C

*WILLY
WILLIES
January-March*

Tropic of Capricorn

Vostok in
Antarctica
Coldest place
on Earth –89°C

Southern
Hemisphere –
WINTER

Paths of
tropical
storms

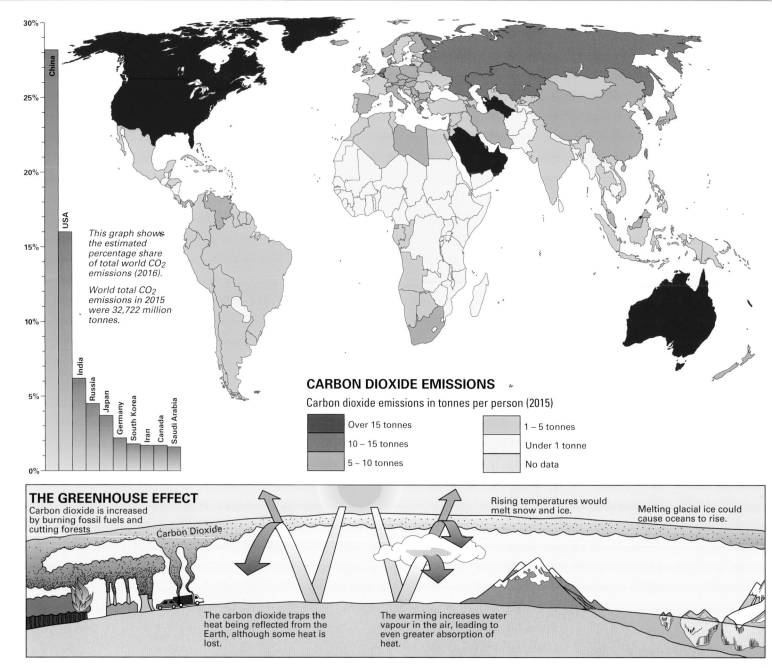

This graph shows the estimated percentage share of total world CO_2 emissions (2016).

World total CO_2 emissions in 2015 were 32,722 million tonnes.

CARBON DIOXIDE EMISSIONS

Carbon dioxide emissions in tonnes per person (2015)

- Over 15 tonnes
- 10 – 15 tonnes
- 5 – 10 tonnes
- 1 – 5 tonnes
- Under 1 tonne
- No data

THE GREENHOUSE EFFECT

Carbon dioxide is increased by burning fossil fuels and cutting forests

Carbon Dioxide

Rising temperatures would melt snow and ice.

Melting glacial ice could cause oceans to rise.

The carbon dioxide traps the heat being reflected from the Earth, although some heat is lost.

The warming increases water vapour in the air, leading to even greater absorption of heat.

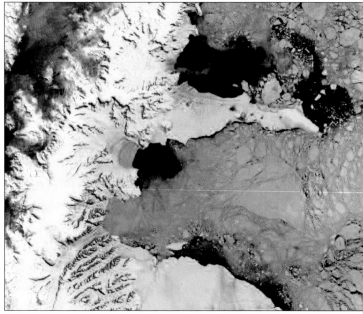

▲ **Larsen B ice shelf, Antarctica.** Between January and March 2002, Larsen B ice shelf on the Antarctic Peninsula collapsed. The image on the left shows its area before the collapse, while the image on the right shows the area after the collapse. The 200 m thick ice sheet had been retreating before this date, but over 500 billion tonnes of ice collapsed in under a month. This was due to rising temperatures of 0.5°C per year in this part of Antarctica. Satellite images like these are the only way for scientists to monitor inaccessible areas of the world.

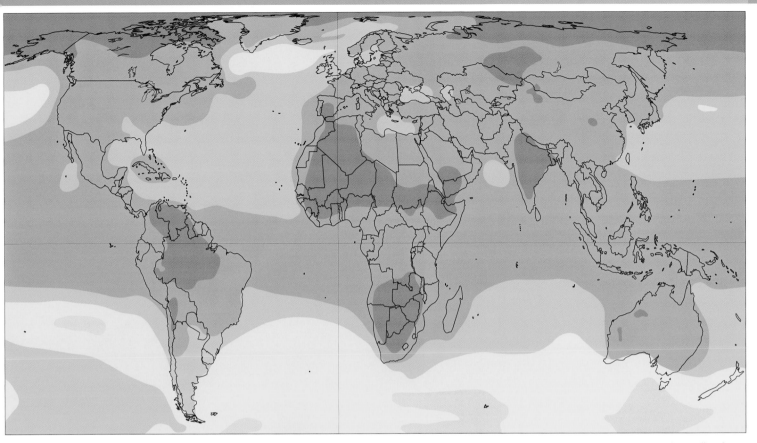

PREDICTED CHANGE IN TEMPERATURE

The difference between actual annual average surface air temperature, 1969–1990, and predicted annual average surface air temperature, 2070–2100

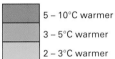

5 – 10°C warmer	1 – 2°C warmer
3 – 5°C warmer	0 – 1°C warmer
2 – 3°C warmer	

These maps shows the predicted increase assuming a 'medium growth' of the global economy and assuming that no measures to combat the emission of greenhouse gases are taken.

It should be noted that these predicted annual average changes mask quite significant seasonal detail.

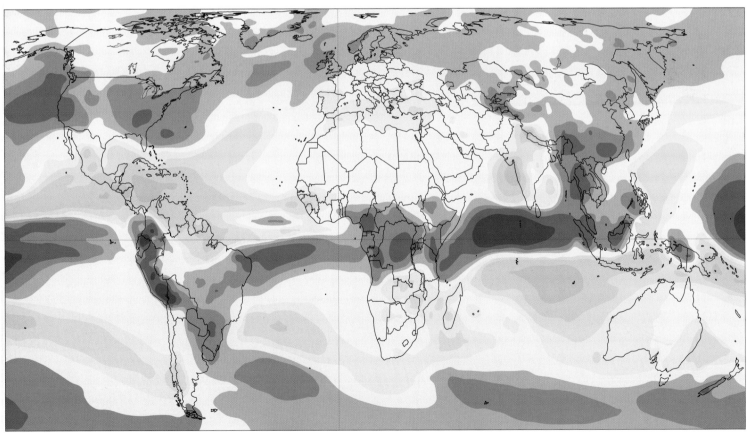

PREDICTED CHANGE IN RAINFALL

The difference between actual annual average rainfall, 1969–1990, and predicted annual average rainfall, 2070–2100

Over 2 mm more rain per day	0.2 – 0.5 mm more rain per day	0.5 – 1 mm less rain per day
1 – 2 mm more rain per day	No change	1 – 2 mm less rain per day
Over 2 mm more rain per day	0.2 – 0.5 mm less rain per day	Over 2 mm less rain per day

Source: The Hadley Centre of Climate Prediction and Research, Met Office

TUNDRA AND MOUNTAIN VEGETATION

NEEDLELEAF EVERGREEN FOREST

MID-LATITUDE GRASSLAND

TROPICAL BROADLEAF RAINFOREST

DESERT

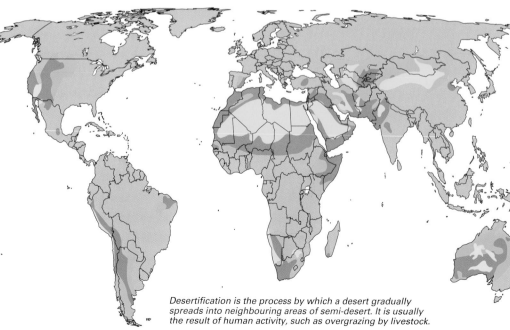

Desertification is the process by which a desert gradually spreads into neighbouring areas of semi-desert. It is usually the result of human activity, such as overgrazing by livestock.

DESERTIFICATION

Existing desert

Areas with a high risk of desertification

Areas with a moderate risk of desertification

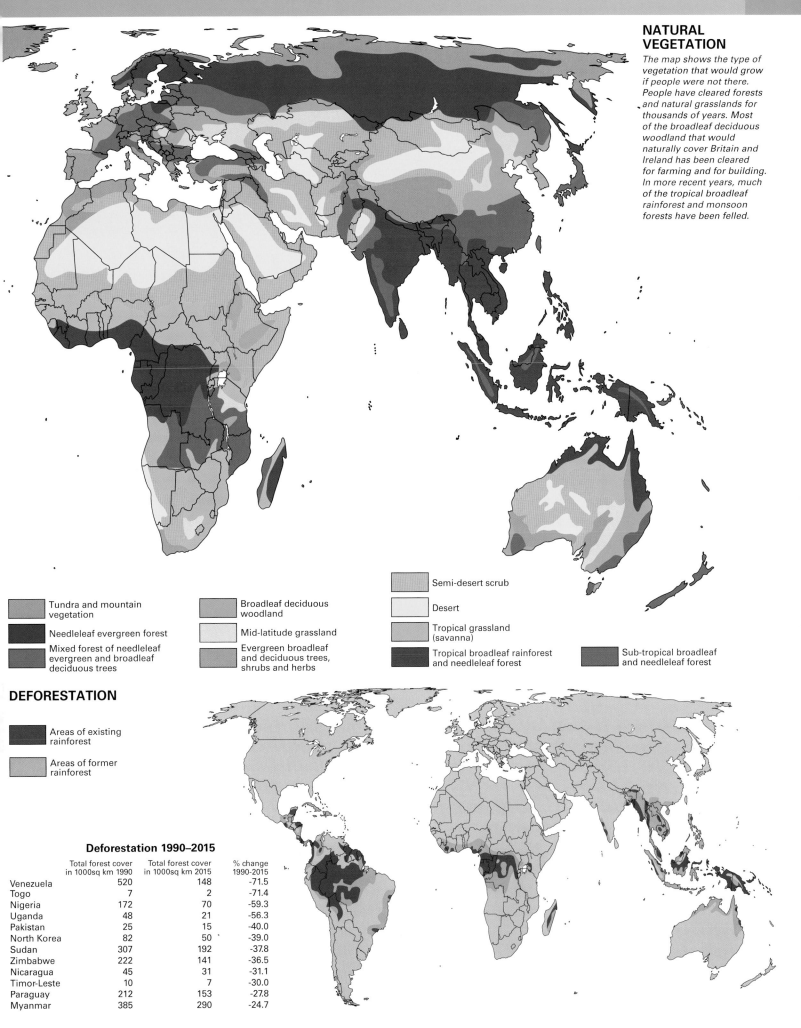

NATURAL VEGETATION

The map shows the type of vegetation that would grow if people were not there. People have cleared forests and natural grasslands for thousands of years. Most of the broadleaf deciduous woodland that would naturally cover Britain and Ireland has been cleared for farming and for building. In more recent years, much of the tropical broadleaf rainforest and monsoon forests have been felled.

Legend (Natural Vegetation):
- Tundra and mountain vegetation
- Needleleaf evergreen forest
- Mixed forest of needleleaf evergreen and broadleaf deciduous trees
- Broadleaf deciduous woodland
- Mid-latitude grassland
- Evergreen broadleaf and deciduous trees, shrubs and herbs
- Semi-desert scrub
- Desert
- Tropical grassland (savanna)
- Tropical broadleaf rainforest and needleleaf forest
- Sub-tropical broadleaf and needleleaf forest

DEFORESTATION

- Areas of existing rainforest
- Areas of former rainforest

Deforestation 1990–2015

	Total forest cover in 1000sq km 1990	Total forest cover in 1000sq km 2015	% change 1990-2015
Venezuela	520	148	-71.5
Togo	7	2	-71.4
Nigeria	172	70	-59.3
Uganda	48	21	-56.3
Pakistan	25	15	-40.0
North Korea	82	50	-39.0
Sudan	307	192	-37.8
Zimbabwe	222	141	-36.5
Nicaragua	45	31	-31.1
Timor-Leste	10	7	-30.0
Paraguay	212	153	-27.8
Myanmar	385	290	-24.7

CONTINENTAL DRIFT

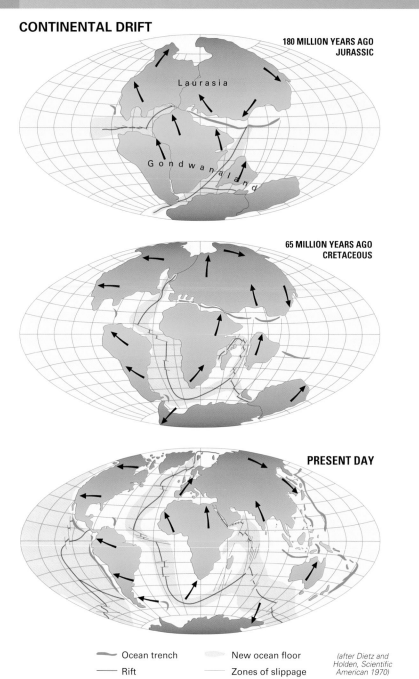

**180 MILLION YEARS AGO
JURASSIC**

Laurasia

Gondwanaland

**65 MILLION YEARS AGO
CRETACEOUS**

PRESENT DAY

— Ocean trench　　New ocean floor
— Rift　　　　　　 Zones of slippage

(after Dietz and Holden, Scientific American 1970)

▲ In 1995, after almost 400 years lying dormant, the Soufrière Hills volcano on the Caribbean island of Montserrat began a series of eruptions. Further eruptions in 1996 and 1997 left the south of the island uninhabitable and 5,000 people had to be evacuated to the northern zone. Steam can be seen rising from the volcano in the false colour satellite image, above.

SOUFRIÈRE HILLS VOLCANO, MONTSERRAT

403 ▲

NORTHERN ZONE
(low risk of ash flow)

Brades (current capital)

St. John's

St. Peter's

➡ Pyroclastic (ash) flow

Areas at most risk from effects of eruption

Risk zone boundaries in September 1997

CENTRAL ZONE
(controlled access)

739 ▲

Salem

Bethel

Soufrière Hills
▲ 914

Plymouth
(former capital)

754 ▲

EXCLUSION ZONE
(enforced evacuation)

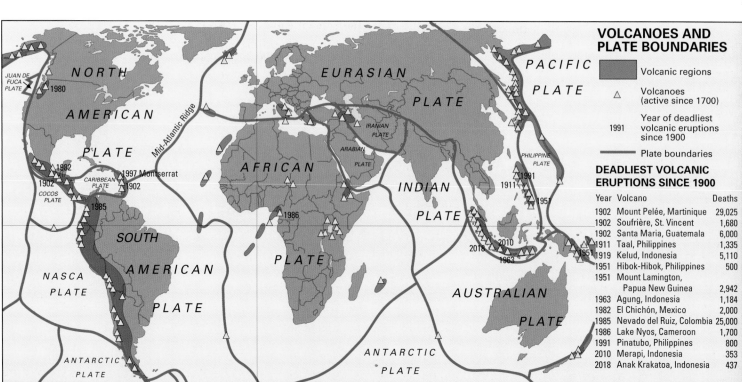

VOLCANOES AND PLATE BOUNDARIES

Volcanic regions

△ Volcanoes (active since 1700)

1991　Year of deadliest volcanic eruptions since 1900

— Plate boundaries

DEADLIEST VOLCANIC ERUPTIONS SINCE 1900

Year	Volcano	Deaths
1902	Mount Pelée, Martinique	29,025
1902	Soufrière, St. Vincent	1,680
1902	Santa Maria, Guatemala	6,000
1911	Taal, Philippines	1,335
1919	Kelud, Indonesia	5,110
1951	Hibok-Hibok, Philippines	500
1951	Mount Lamington, Papua New Guinea	2,942
1963	Agung, Indonesia	1,184
1982	El Chichón, Mexico	2,000
1985	Nevado del Ruiz, Colombia	25,000
1986	Lake Nyos, Cameroon	1,700
1991	Pinatubo, Philippines	800
2010	Merapi, Indonesia	353
2018	Anak Krakatau, Indonesia	437

NORTH AMERICAN PLATE

JUAN DE FUCA PLATE

1980

EURASIAN PLATE

PACIFIC PLATE

Mid-Atlantic Ridge

IRANIAN PLATE

ARABIAN PLATE

PHILIPPINE PLATE

1982

1997 Montserrat

CARIBBEAN PLATE

1902

1902

COCOS PLATE

1985

AFRICAN PLATE

1991

1911

1951

INDIAN PLATE

SOUTH AMERICAN PLATE

1986

2018

2010

1963

1951

NASCA PLATE

PLATE

AUSTRALIAN PLATE

ANTARCTIC PLATE

ANTARCTIC PLATE

COPYRIGHT PHILIP'S

PLATE TECTONICS IN THE CARIBBEAN

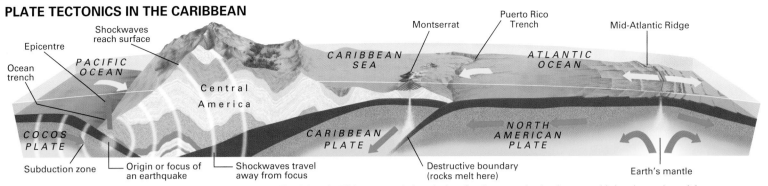

The North American Plate is moving away from the Mid-Atlantic Ridge and towards the Caribbean Plate at a rate of 30-40mm a year. The edge of the North American Plate is forced downwards under the Caribbean Plate. As the North American Plate descends, the rocks melt and are destroyed. This is called a *destructive boundary*. The destructive boundary to the east of the Caribbean has caused the Puerto Rico Trench and the chain of volcanoes in the Leeward Islands such as Montserrat. The molten rocks along the destructive boundary are forced upwards through cracks at the edge of the Caribbean Plate to pour out as lava from volcanoes. Earthquakes are also common along destructive plate boundaries, as is the case in Central America, along the boundary between the Caribbean and Cocos Plates.

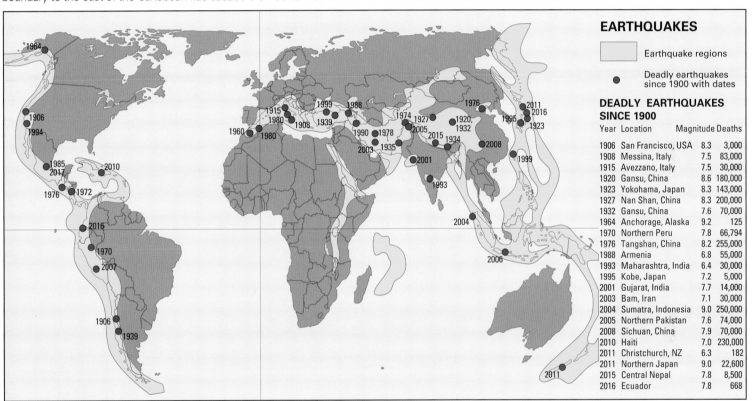

EARTHQUAKES

☐ Earthquake regions

● Deadly earthquakes since 1900 with dates

DEADLY EARTHQUAKES SINCE 1900

Year	Location	Magnitude	Deaths
1906	San Francisco, USA	8.3	3,000
1908	Messina, Italy	7.5	83,000
1915	Avezzano, Italy	7.5	30,000
1920	Gansu, China	8.6	180,000
1923	Yokohama, Japan	8.3	143,000
1927	Nan Shan, China	8.3	200,000
1932	Gansu, China	7.6	70,000
1964	Anchorage, Alaska	9.2	125
1970	Northern Peru	7.8	66,794
1976	Tangshan, China	8.2	255,000
1988	Armenia	6.8	55,000
1993	Maharashtra, India	6.4	30,000
1995	Kobe, Japan	7.2	5,000
2001	Gujarat, India	7.7	14,000
2003	Bam, Iran	7.1	30,000
2004	Sumatra, Indonesia	9.0	250,000
2005	Northern Pakistan	7.6	74,000
2008	Sichuan, China	7.9	70,000
2010	Haiti	7.0	230,000
2011	Christchurch, NZ	6.3	182
2011	Northern Japan	9.0	22,600
2015	Central Nepal	7.8	8,500
2016	Ecuador	7.8	668

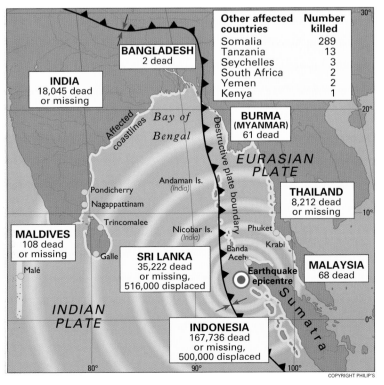

Other affected countries	Number killed
Somalia	289
Tanzania	13
Seychelles	3
South Africa	2
Yemen	2
Kenya	1

INDIAN OCEAN TSUNAMI

On 26 December 2004, an earthquake off the coast of Sumatra triggered a deadly tsunami that swept across the Indian Ocean, causing devastation in many countries (see map left).

The image below shows the turbulent receding waters of the tsunami, on the west coast of Sri Lanka. Such imagery enabled rescuers to assess the worst affected areas.

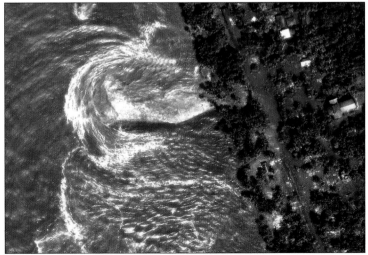

COPYRIGHT PHILIP'S

POPULATION DENSITY BY COUNTRY

Density of people per square kilometre (2018)

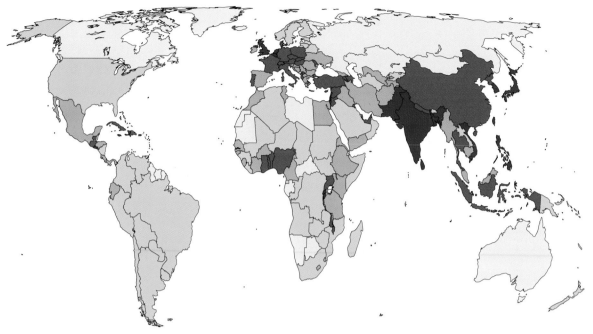

■	250 per km² and over
■	100 – 250 per km²
■	50 – 100 per km²
■	10 – 50 per km²
□	Under 10 per km²
□	No data

Most and least densely populated countries

Most per km²		Least per km²	
Singapore	8,818	Mongolia	2
Bahrain	2,091	Namibia	3
Malta	1,403	Iceland	3
Maldives	1,308	Guyana	3
Bangladesh	1,107	Australia	3

UK 269 per km²

POPULATION CHANGE

Expected change in total population (2004–2050)

■	Over 125% gain
■	100 – 125% gain
■	50 – 100% gain
□	25 – 50% gain
□	0 – 25% gain
□	No change or loss

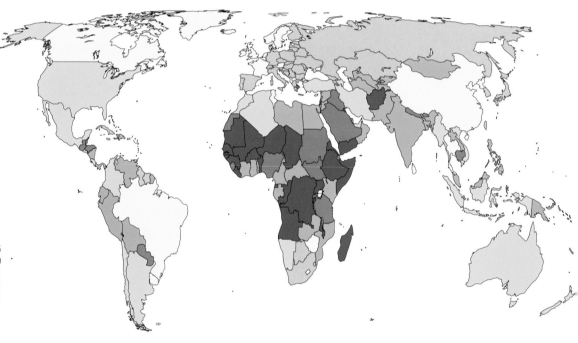

Based on estimates for the year 2050, the ten most populous nations in the world will be, in millions:

India	1,628	Pakistan	295
China	1,437	Bangladesh	280
USA	420	Brazil	221
Indonesia	308	Congo Dem. Rep.	181
Nigeria	307	Ethiopia	171

UK (2050) 77 million

URBAN POPULATION

Percentage of total population living in towns and cities (2018)

■	80% urban and over
■	60 – 80% urban
■	40 – 60% urban
□	20 – 40% urban
□	Under 20% urban
□	No data

Countries that are the most and least urbanized (%)

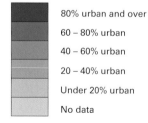

Most urbanized		Least urbanized	
Kuwait	100	Burundi	13
Monaco	100	Papua N. Guinea	13
Singapore	100	Liechtenstein	14

UK 83% urban

In 2008, for the first time in history, more than half the world's population lived in urban areas.

POPULATION BY CONTINENT

In this diagram the size of each continent is in proportion to its population (2015).

Each square represents 10 million people.

Population of countries (2018)
Top 20 countries (millions)

Country	Population
China	1,385
India	1,297
USA	329
Indonesia	263
Brazil	209
Pakistan	208
Nigeria	204
Bangladesh	160
Russia	142
Japan	126
Mexico	126
Ethiopia	108
Philippines	106
Egypt	99
Vietnam	97
Congo, Dem. Rep.	85
Iran	83
Turkey	81
Germany	81
Thailand	69

UK 65 million

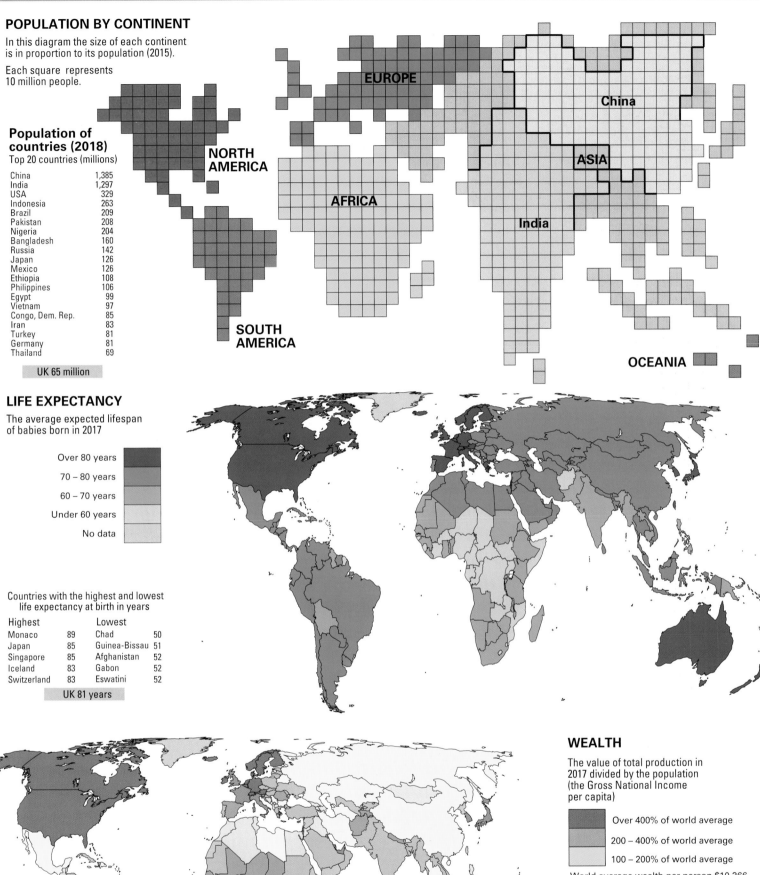

EUROPE

China

NORTH AMERICA

AFRICA

ASIA

India

SOUTH AMERICA

OCEANIA

LIFE EXPECTANCY

The average expected lifespan of babies born in 2017

- Over 80 years
- 70 – 80 years
- 60 – 70 years
- Under 60 years
- No data

Countries with the highest and lowest life expectancy at birth in years

Highest		Lowest	
Monaco	89	Chad	50
Japan	85	Guinea-Bissau	51
Singapore	85	Afghanistan	52
Iceland	83	Gabon	52
Switzerland	83	Eswatini	52

UK 81 years

WEALTH

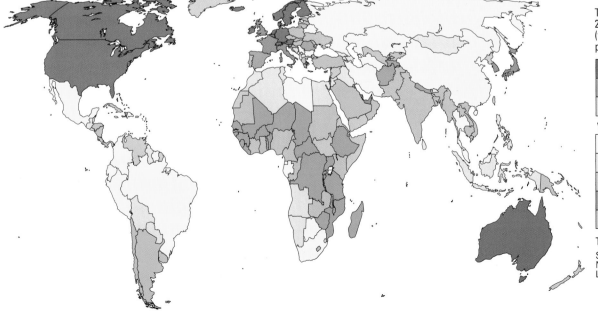

The value of total production in 2017 divided by the population (the Gross National Income per capita)

- Over 400% of world average
- 200 – 400% of world average
- 100 – 200% of world average

World average wealth per person $10,366

- 50 – 100% of world average
- 25 – 50% of world average
- 10 – 25% of world average
- Under 10% of world average
- No data

Top 3 countries		Bottom 3 countries	
Switzerland	$80,560	Burundi	$290
Norway	$75,990	Malawi	$320
Luxembourg	$70,260	Niger	$360

UK $40,530

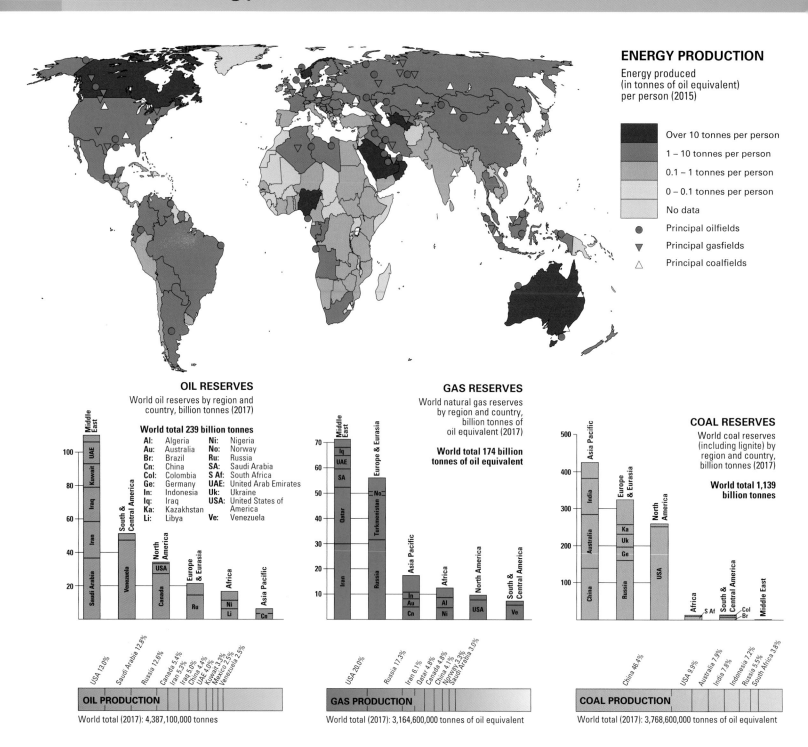

ENERGY PRODUCTION

Energy produced
(in tonnes of oil equivalent)
per person (2015)

- Over 10 tonnes per person
- 1 – 10 tonnes per person
- 0.1 – 1 tonnes per person
- 0 – 0.1 tonnes per person
- No data
- ● Principal oilfields
- ▼ Principal gasfields
- △ Principal coalfields

OIL RESERVES

World oil reserves by region and
country, billion tonnes (2017)

World total 239 billion tonnes

Al: Algeria	**Ni:** Nigeria
Au: Australia	**No:** Norway
Br: Brazil	**Ru:** Russia
Cn: China	**SA:** Saudi Arabia
Col: Colombia	**S Af:** South Africa
Ge: Germany	**UAE:** United Arab Emirates
In: Indonesia	**Uk:** Ukraine
Iq: Iraq	**USA:** United States of America
Ka: Kazakhstan	
Li: Libya	**Ve:** Venezuela

OIL PRODUCTION

USA 13.0%
Saudi Arabia 12.8%
Russia 12.6%
Canada 5.4%
Iran 5.3%
Iraq 5.0%
China 4.4%
UAE 4.0%
Kuwait 3.3%
Mexico 2.5%
Venezuela 2.5%

World total (2017): 4,387,100,000 tonnes

GAS RESERVES

World natural gas reserves
by region and country,
billion tonnes of
oil equivalent (2017)

**World total 174 billion
tonnes of oil equivalent**

GAS PRODUCTION

USA 20.0%
Russia 17.3%
Iran 6.1%
Qatar 4.8%
Canada 4.8%
China 4.1%
Norway 3.3%
Saudi Arabia 3.0%

World total (2017): 3,164,600,000 tonnes of oil equivalent

COAL RESERVES

World coal reserves
(including lignite) by
region and country,
billion tonnes (2017)

**World total 1,139
billion tonnes**

COAL PRODUCTION

China 46.4%
USA 9.9%
Australia 7.9%
India 7.8%
Indonesia 7.2%
Russia 5.5%
South Africa 3.8%

World total (2017): 3,768,600,000 tonnes of oil equivalent

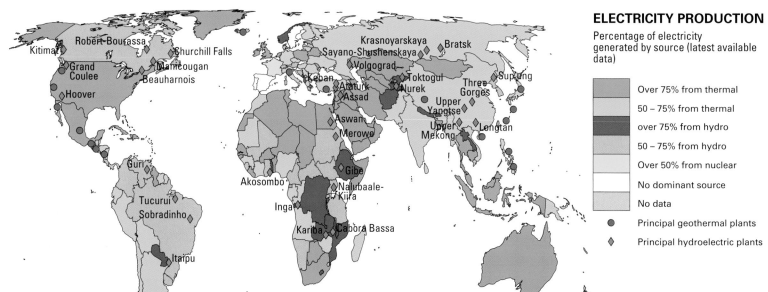

ELECTRICITY PRODUCTION

Percentage of electricity
generated by source (latest available
data)

- Over 75% from thermal
- 50 – 75% from thermal
- over 75% from hydro
- 50 – 75% from hydro
- Over 50% from nuclear
- No dominant source
- No data
- ● Principal geothermal plants
- ◆ Principal hydroelectric plants

FOOD PRODUCTION

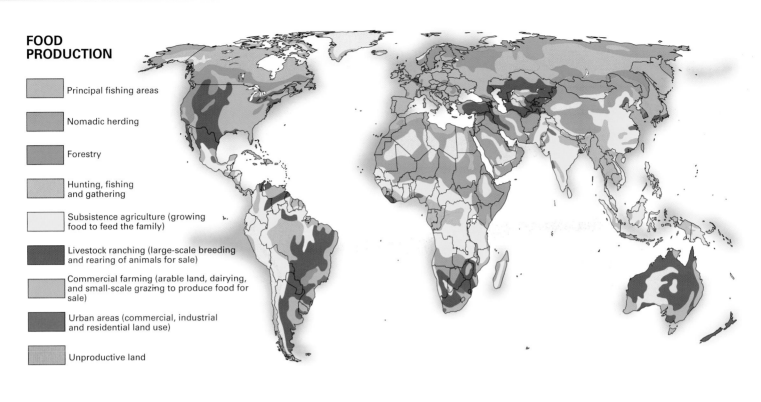

- Principal fishing areas
- Nomadic herding
- Forestry
- Hunting, fishing and gathering
- Subsistence agriculture (growing food to feed the family)
- Livestock ranching (large-scale breeding and rearing of animals for sale)
- Commercial farming (arable land, dairying, and small-scale grazing to produce food for sale)
- Urban areas (commercial, industrial and residential land use)
- Unproductive land

LEVEL OF OBESITY

Percentage of total adult population considered to be obese*

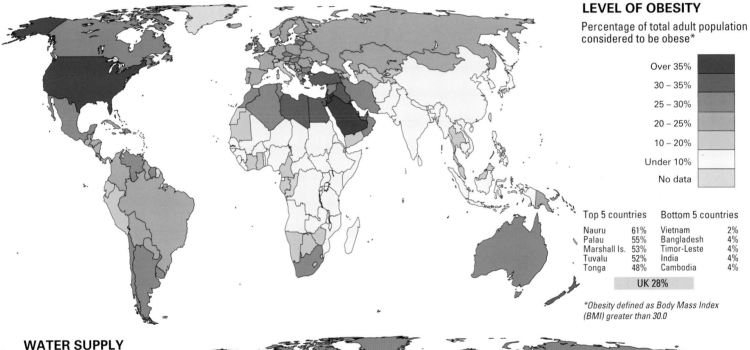

- Over 35%
- 30 – 35%
- 25 – 30%
- 20 – 25%
- 10 – 20%
- Under 10%
- No data

Top 5 countries		Bottom 5 countries	
Nauru	61%	Vietnam	2%
Palau	55%	Bangladesh	4%
Marshall Is.	53%	Timor-Leste	4%
Tuvalu	52%	India	4%
Tonga	48%	Cambodia	4%

UK 28%

Obesity defined as Body Mass Index (BMI) greater than 30.0

WATER SUPPLY

The percentage of total population with access to safe drinking water

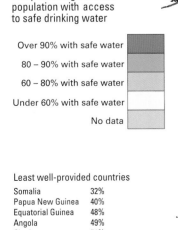

- Over 90% with safe water
- 80 – 90% with safe water
- 60 – 80% with safe water
- Under 60% with safe water
- No data

Least well-provided countries

Somalia	32%
Papua New Guinea	40%
Equatorial Guinea	48%
Angola	49%
Chad	51%
Mozambique	51%

One person in eight in the world has no access to a safe water supply.

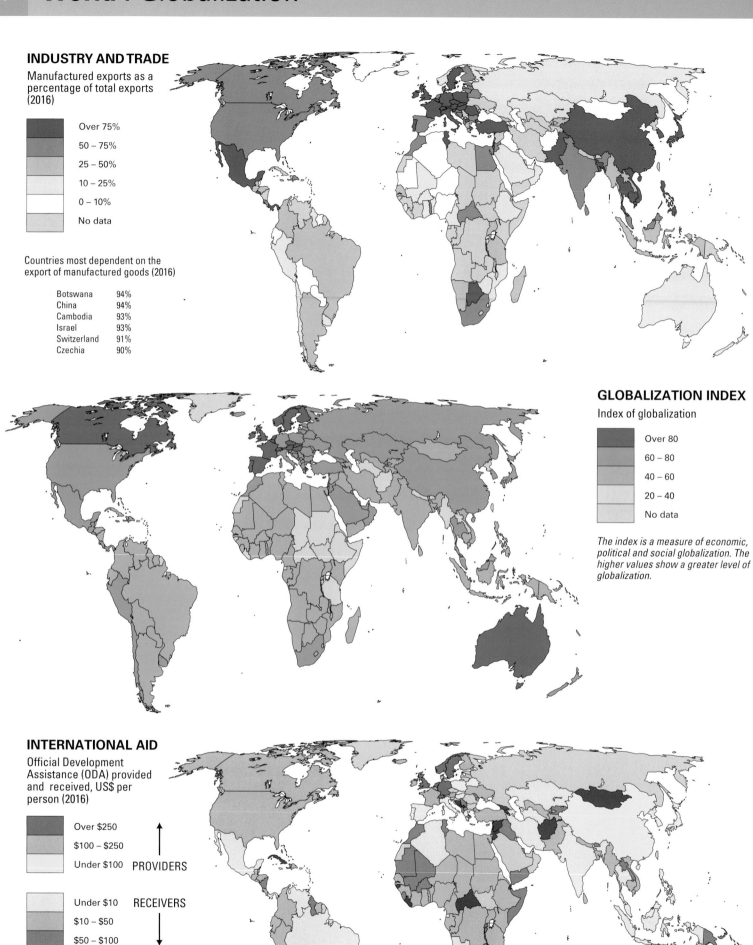

INDUSTRY AND TRADE

Manufactured exports as a percentage of total exports (2016)

- Over 75%
- 50 – 75%
- 25 – 50%
- 10 – 25%
- 0 – 10%
- No data

Countries most dependent on the export of manufactured goods (2016)

Botswana	94%
China	94%
Cambodia	93%
Israel	93%
Switzerland	91%
Czechia	90%

GLOBALIZATION INDEX

Index of globalization

- Over 80
- 60 – 80
- 40 – 60
- 20 – 40
- No data

The index is a measure of economic, political and social globalization. The higher values show a greater level of globalization.

INTERNATIONAL AID

Official Development Assistance (ODA) provided and received, US$ per person (2016)

- Over $250
- $100 – $250
- Under $100   PROVIDERS ↑

- Under $10   RECEIVERS ↓
- $10 – $50
- $50 – $100
- Over $100
- No data

Top 5 providers		Top 5 receivers	
Norway	$832	Tuvalu	$3,034
Luxembourg	$671	Nauru	$1,796
Sweden	$495	Palau	$823
Switzerland	$438	Tonga	$744
Germany	$306	Kiribati	$553

UK provides $280

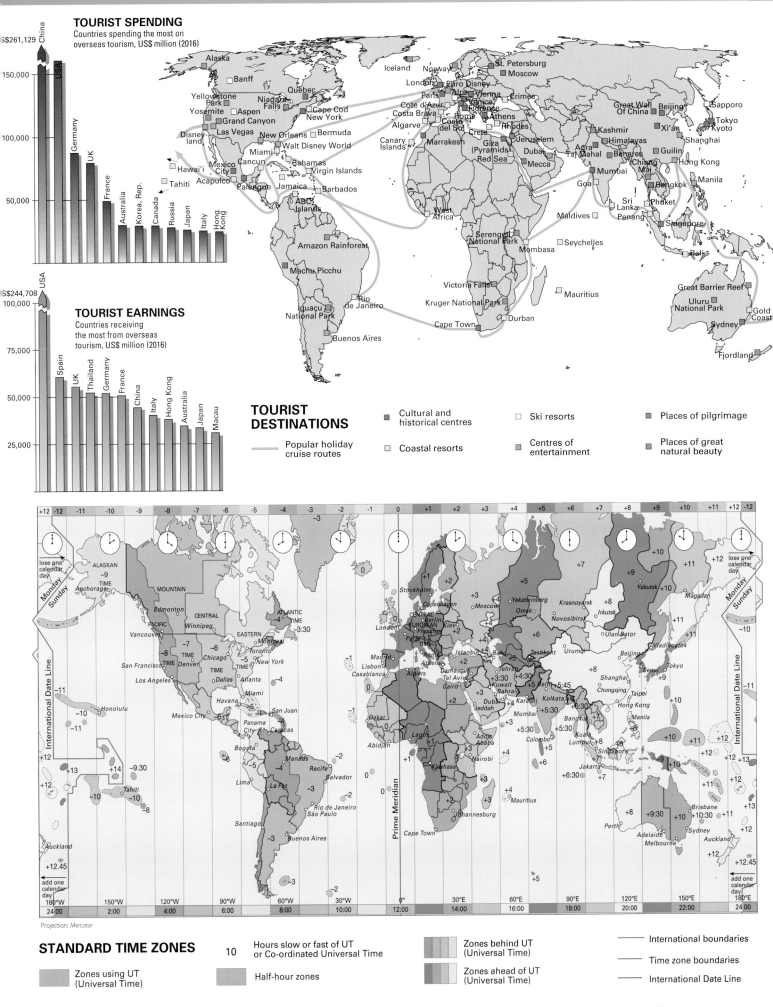

TOURIST SPENDING

Countries spending the most on overseas tourism, US$ million (2016)

US$261,129 China

TOURIST EARNINGS

Countries receiving the most from overseas tourism, US$ million (2016)

US$244,708 USA

TOURIST DESTINATIONS

— Popular holiday cruise routes

- ■ Cultural and historical centres
- □ Coastal resorts
- □ Ski resorts
- ■ Centres of entertainment
- ■ Places of pilgrimage
- ■ Places of great natural beauty

Projection: Mercator

STANDARD TIME ZONES

10   Hours slow or fast of UT or Co-ordinated Universal Time

▨ Zones using UT (Universal Time)

▨ Half-hour zones

▨ Zones behind UT (Universal Time)

▨ Zones ahead of UT (Universal Time)

— International boundaries

— Time zone boundaries

— International Date Line

The Earth rotates through 360° in 24 hours, and so moves 15° every hour. The World is divided into 24 standard time zones, each centred on lines of longitude at 15° intervals. The Greenwich Meridian (or Prime Meridian) lies on the centre of the first zone. All places to the west of Greenwich are one hour behind for every 15° of longitude; places to the east are ahead by one hour for every 15°.

FLAG	COUNTRY	CAPITAL CITY	AREA thousand square kilometres 2018	POPULATION in millions 2018	POPULATION CHANGE percent per year 2018	BIRTHS per thousand people 2018	DEATHS per thousand people 2018	LIFE EXPECTANCY years 2018	INCOME US $ per person 2017
	Afghanistan	Kabul	652	34.9	2.3	37	13	52	2,000
	Albania	Tirane	28.7	3.0	0.3	13	7	78	12,500
	Algeria	Algiers	2,382	41.6	1.6	21	4	77	15,200
	Angola	Luanda	1,247	30.3	3.4	44	9	60	6,800
	Argentina	Buenos Aires	2,780	44.7	0.9	16	7	77	20,900
	Armenia	Yerevan	29.8	3.0	-0.2	13	9	75	9,500
	Australia	Canberra	7,741	23.5	1.0	12	7	82	50,400
	Austria	Vienna	83.9	8.8	0.4	9	10	81	50,000
	Azerbaijan	Baku	86.6	10.1	0.8	15	7	73	17,500
	Bahamas	Nassau	13.9	0.3	0.8	15	7	73	32,400
	Bahrain	Manama	0.7	1.4	2.1	13	3	79	49,000
	Bangladesh	Dhaka	144	159.4	1.0	19	5	73	4,200
	Barbados	Bridgetown	0.4	0.3	0.3	12	9	75	18,600
	Belarus	Minsk	208	9.5	-0.2	10	13	73	18,900
	Belgium	Brussels	30.5	11.5	0.7	11	10	81	46,600
	Belize	Belmopan	23.0	0.4	1.8	23	4	74	8,300
	Benin	Porto-Novo	113	11.3	2.6	34	8	62	2,300
	Bhutan	Thimphu	47.0	0.8	1.1	17	6	71	9,000
	Bolivia	La Paz/Sucre	1,099	11.3	1.5	22	6	69	7,600
	Bosnia-Herzegovina	Sarajevo	51.2	3.8	-0.2	9	10	77	12,800
	Botswana	Gaborone	582	2.2	1.5	22	9	63	17,000
	Brazil	Brasília	8,514	208.8	0.7	14	7	74	15,600
	Brunei	Bandar Seri Begawan	5.8	0.4	1.5	17	4	77	78,900
	Bulgaria	Sofia	111	7.0	-0.6	9	14	74	21,800
	Burkina Faso	Ouagadougou	274	19.7	2.7	37	9	61	1,900
	Burundi	Bujumbura	27.8	11.8	3.2	41	9	61	700
	Cabo Verde	Praia	4.0	0.5	1.3	20	6	72	7,000
	Cambodia	Phnom Penh	181	16.4	1.4	22	7	65	4,000
	Cameroon	Yaoundé	475	25.6	2.5	35	9	59	3,700
	Canada	Ottawa	9,971	35.8	0.7	10	9	82	48,400
	Central African Republic	Bangui	623	5.7	2.1	34	13	53	700
	Chad	N'djamena	1,284	15.8	3.2	43	10	57	2,300
	Chile	Santiago	757	17.9	0.7	13	6	79	24,600
	China	Beijing	9,597	1,384.7	0.4	12	8	75	16,700
	Colombia	Bogotá	1,139	48.1	1.0	16	5	76	14,400
	Congo	Brazzaville	342	5.1	2.2	34	9	60	6,800
	Congo (Dem. Rep.)	Kinshasa	2,345	85.2	2.3	33	9	58	800
	Costa Rica	San José	51.1	4.9	1.1	15	5	78	16,900
	Côte d'Ivoire	Yamoussoukro	322	26.2	2.3	30	8	60	3,900
	Croatia	Zagreb	56.5	4.2	-0.5	9	12	76	24,700
	Cuba	Havana	111	11.1	-0.2	11	9	78	12,300
	Cyprus	Nicosia	9.3	1.2	1.2	11	7	79	37,200
	Czechia	Prague	78.9	10.6	0.1	9	10	78	35,500

FLAG	COUNTRY	CAPITAL CITY	AREA thousand square kilometres 2018	POPULATION in millions 2018	POPULATION CHANGE percent per year 2018	BIRTHS per thousand people 2018	DEATHS per thousand people 2018	LIFE EXPECTANCY years 2018	INCOME US $ per person 2017
	Denmark	Copenhagen	43.1	5.8	0.6	11	9	81	50,100
	Djibouti	Djibouti	23.2	0.9	2.1	23	7	64	3,600
	Dominican Republic	Santo Domingo	48.5	10.3	1.0	19	6	71	17,000
	Ecuador	Quito	284	16.5	1.2	18	5	77	11,500
	Egypt	Cairo	1,001	99.4	2.4	29	4	73	12,700
	El Salvador	San Salvador	21.0	6.1	0.3	16	6	75	8,000
	Equatorial Guinea	Malabo	28.1	0.8	2.4	32	8	65	37,400
	Eritrea	Asmara	118	6.0	0.9	29	7	65	1,600
	Estonia	Tallinn	45.1	1.2	-0.6	10	13	77	31,700
	Eswatini	Mbabane	17.4	1.0	0.8	26	11	57	10,100
	Ethiopia	Addis Ababa	1,104	108.3	2.8	36	7	63	2,200
	Fiji	Suva	18.3	0.9	0.6	18	6	73	9,800
	Finland	Helsinki	338	5.5	0.3	11	10	81	44,500
	France	Paris	552	67.3	0.4	12	9	82	44,100
	Gabon	Libreville	268	2.1	2.7	26	6	68	18,100
	Gambia	Banjul	11.3	2.0	2.0	29	6	65	2,600
	Georgia	Tbilisi	69.7	4.9	0.0	12	11	76	10,700
	Germany	Berlin	357	80.4	-0.2	9	12	81	50,800
	Ghana	Accra	239	28.1	2.1	30	7	67	4,700
	Greece	Athens	132	10.8	0.0	8	11	80	27,800
	Guatemala	Guatemala	109	16.5	1.7	25	5	72	8,200
	Guinea	Conakry	246	11.8	2.7	36	9	62	2,200
	Guinea-Bissau	Bissau	36.1	1.8	2.4	37	8	61	1,900
	Guyana	Georgetown	215	0.7	0.5	15	7	68	8,100
	Haiti	Port-au-Prince	27.8	10.7	1.3	23	7	64	1,800
	Honduras	Tegucigalpa	112	9.1	1.6	22	5	71	4,300
	Hungary	Budapest	93.0	9.8	-0.3	9	13	76	29,600
	Iceland	Reykjavik	103	0.3	1.0	14	6	83	52,200
	India	New Delhi	3,287	1,296.8	1.1	19	7	69	7,200
	Indonesia	Jakarta	1,905	262.7	0.8	16	6	73	12,400
	Iran	Tehrān	1,648	83.4	1.2	17	6	74	20,100
	Iraq	Baghdād	438	40.1	2.5	30	4	74	16,700
	Ireland	Dublin	70.3	5.1	1.1	14	7	81	73,200
	Israel	Jerusalem	20.6	8.4	1.5	18	5	82	36,400
	Italy	Rome	301	62.2	0.2	8	10	82	38,200
	Jamaica	Kingston	11.0	2.8	0.0	17	8	74	9,200
	Japan	Tokyo	378	126.1	0.0	8	10	85	42,900
	Jordan	Amman	89.3	10.4	2.0	24	3	75	9,200
	Kazakhstan	Astana	2,725	18.7	0.9	17	8	71	26,300
	Kenya	Nairobi	580	48.4	1.6	23	7	64	3,500
	Korea, North	P'yŏngyang	121	25.4	0.5	15	9	71	1,700
	Korea, South	Seoul	99.3	51.4	0.4	8	6	82	39,500
	Kosovo	Priština	10.9	1.9	0.0	16	7	72	10,900

FLAG	COUNTRY	CAPITAL CITY	AREA thousand square kilometres 2018	POPULATION in millions 2018	POPULATION CHANGE percent per year 2018	BIRTHS per thousand people 2018	DEATHS per thousand people 2018	LIFE EXPECTANCY years 2018	INCOME US $ per person 2017
	Kuwait	Kuwait	17.8	2.9	1.3	19	2	78	65,800
	Kyrgyzstan	Bishkek	200	5.8	1.0	22	6	71	3,700
	Laos	Vientiane	237	7.2	1.5	23	7	65	7,400
	Latvia	Riga	64.6	1.9	-1.1	10	14	74	27,700
	Lebanon	Beirut	10.4	6.1	-3.1	14	5	77	19,600
	Lesotho	Maseru	30.4	1.9	0.2	24	15	53	3,300
	Liberia	Monrovia	111	4.8	2.6	38	7	63	1,300
	Libya	Tripoli	1,760	6.7	1.4	17	4	76	9,600
	Lithuania	Vilnius	65.2	2.8	-1.1	10	15	75	32,400
	Luxembourg	Luxembourg	2.6	0.6	1.9	12	7	82	105,100
	Macedonia	Skopje	25.7	2.1	0.2	11	9	75	14,900
	Madagascar	Antananarivo	587	25.6	2.5	31	6	66	1,600
	Malawi	Lilongwe	118	19.8	3.3	41	8	62	1,200
	Malaysia	Kuala Lumpur/ Putrajaya	330	31.8	1.3	19	5	75	29,100
	Mali	Bamako	1,240	18.4	3.0	43	10	60	2,200
	Malta	Valletta	0.3	0.4	0.1	10	8	82	41,900
	Mauritania	Nouakchott	1,026	3.8	2.1	30	8	63	4,500
	Mauritius	Port Louis	2.0	1.4	0.6	13	7	76	22,300
	Mexico	Mexico City	1,958	125.9	1.1	18	5	76	19,900
	Moldova	Kishinev	33.9	3.4	-1.0	11	13	71	6,700
	Mongolia	Ulan Bator	1,567	3.1	1.1	18	6	70	13,000
	Montenegro	Podgorica	14.0	0.6	-0.3	12	10	76	17,800
	Morocco	Rabat	447	34.3	1.0	17	5	77	8,600
	Mozambique	Maputo	802	27.2	2.5	38	11	54	1,300
	Myanmar	Yangôn/ Naypyidaw	677	55.6	0.9	18	7	68	6,300
	Namibia	Windhoek	824	2.5	1.9	27	8	64	11,200
	Nepal	Katmandu	147	29.7	1.1	19	6	71	2,700
	Netherlands	Amsterdam/ The Hague	41.5	17.1	0.4	11	9	81	53,900
	New Zealand	Wellington	271	4.5	0.8	13	8	81	39,000
	Nicaragua	Managua	130	6.0	1.0	17	5	73	5,900
	Niger	Niamey	1,267	19.8	3.2	44	11	56	1,200
	Nigeria	Abuja	924	203.4	2.5	35	10	59	5,900
	Norway	Oslo	324	5.3	1.0	12	8	82	72,100
	Oman	Muscat	310	3.4	2.0	24	3	75	46,000
	Pakistan	Islamabad	796	207.8	1.4	22	6	68	5,400
	Panama	Panamá	75.5	3.8	1.2	18	5	78	25,400
	Papua New Guinea	Port Moresby	463	7.0	1.7	23	6	67	3,700
	Paraguay	Asunción	407	7.0	1.2	16	5	77	12,800
	Peru	Lima	1,285	31.3	1.0	18	6	74	13,500
	Philippines	Manila	300	105.8	1.6	23	6	69	8,400
	Poland	Warsaw	323	38.4	-0.1	9	10	77	29,600
	Portugal	Lisbon	88.8	10.5	-0.3	8	11	80	30,500
	Qatar	Doha	11.0	2.3	1.9	9	2	79	124,100

FLAG	COUNTRY	CAPITAL CITY	AREA thousand square kilometres 2018	POPULATION in millions 2018	POPULATION CHANGE percent per year 2018	BIRTHS per thousand people 2018	DEATHS per thousand people 2018	LIFE EXPECTANCY years 2018	INCOME US $ per person 2017
	Romania	Bucharest	238	21.4	-0.3	9	12	75	24,600
	Russia	Moscow	17,075	142.1	-0.1	11	13	71	27,900
	Rwanda	Kigali	26.3	12.1	2.3	30	6	64	2,100
	Saudi Arabia	Riyadh	2,150	33.0	1.6	16	3	75	54,500
	Senegal	Dakar	197	15.0	2.4	33	8	62	3,500
	Serbia	Belgrade	77.5	7.0	-0.5	9	14	75	15,100
	Sierra Leone	Freetown	71.7	6.3	2.4	36	10	59	1,600
	Singapore	Singapore	0.7	5.9	1.8	9	3	85	94,100
	Slovakia	Bratislava	49.0	5.4	0.0	10	10	77	33,100
	Slovenia	Ljubljana	20.3	2.1	0.0	9	10	81	34,500
	Solomon Islands	Honiara	28.9	0.7	1.9	24	4	75	2,200
	Somalia	Mogadishu	638	11.2	2.0	39	13	53	-
	South Africa	Cape Town/ Pretoria	1,221	55.3	0.9	20	9	64	13,600
	South Sudan	Juba	620	10.2	-1.1	37	19	58	1,600
	Spain	Madrid	498	49.3	0.7	9	9	81	38,400
	Sri Lanka	Colombo	65.6	22.6	0.7	15	6	77	12,900
	Sudan	Khartoum	1,886	43.1	2.9	34	7	65	4,300
	Suriname	Paramaribo	163	0.6	1.0	16	6	72	14,900
	Sweden	Stockholm	450	10.0	0.8	12	9	82	51,200
	Switzerland	Berne	41.3	8.2	0.7	10	8	82	62,100
	Syria	Damascus	185	19.4	7.73	21	4	75	2,900
	Taiwan	Taipei	36.0	23.5	0.2	8	8	80	50,500
	Tajikistan	Dushanbe	143	8.6	1.6	23	6	68	3,200
	Tanzania	Dodoma	945	55.4	2.7	35	7	63	3,200
	Thailand	Bangkok	513	68.6	0.3	11	8	75	17,900
	Timor-Leste	Dili	14.9	1.3	2.3	33	6	68	6,000
	Togo	Lomé	56.8	8.1	2.6	33	7	65	1,700
	Trinidad and Tobago	Port of Spain	5.1	1.2	-0.2	12	9	73	31,300
	Tunisia	Tunis	164	11.5	0.9	17	6	75	11,900
	Turkey	Ankara	775	81.2	0.5	15	6	75	27,000
	Turkmenistan	Ashkhabad	488	5.4	1.1	19	6	70	18,200
	Uganda	Kampala	241	40.8	3.2	42	10	56	2,400
	Ukraine	Kiev	604	43.9	0.0	10	14	72	8,800
	United Arab Emirates	Abu Dhabi	83.6	9.7	1.4	10	2	78	68,600
	United Kingdom	London	242	65.1	0.5	12	9	80	44,300
	USA	Washington D.C.	9,629	329.2	0.8	12	8	80	59,800
	Uruguay	Montevideo	175	3.3	0.3	13	9	77	22,400
	Uzbekistan	Tashkent	447	30.0	0.9	17	5	74	6,900
	Venezuela	Caracas	912	31.6	1.2	18	5	76	12,500
	Vietnam	Hanoi	332	97.0	1.0	15	6	73	6,900
	Yemen	Sana	528	28.6	2.1	28	6	66	2,500
	Zambia	Lusaka	753	16.4	2.9	41	12	53	4,000
	Zimbabwe	Harare	391	14.0	1.9	34	10	61	2,300

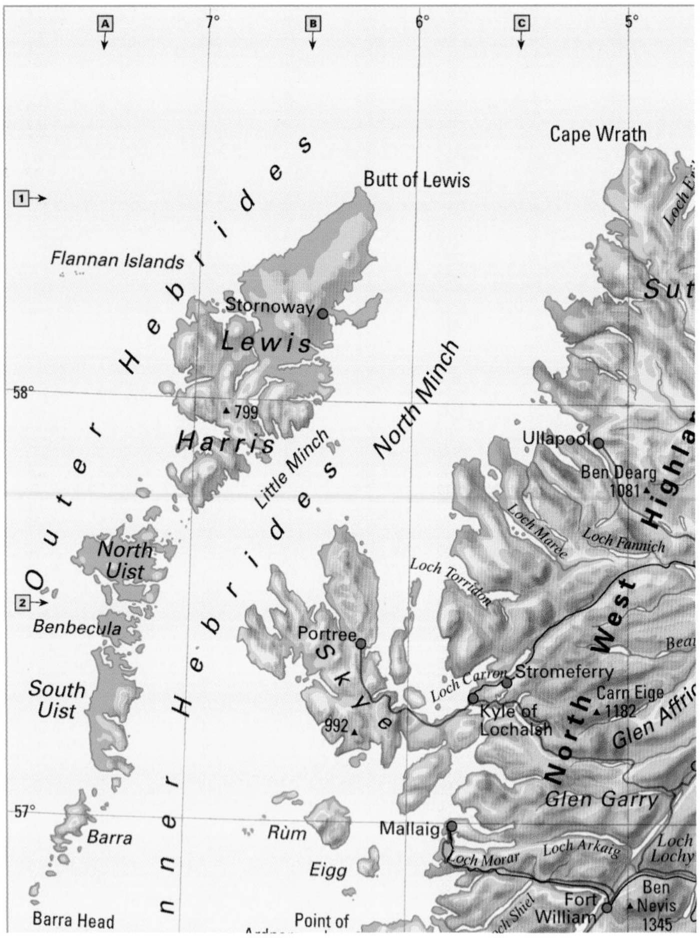

This index contains the names of all the principal places and features shown on the maps in the atlas. They are listed in alphabetical order. If a name has a description as part of it, for example, Bay of Biscay, the name is in alphabetical order, followed by the description:

Biscay, Bay of . . . . . .

Sometimes, the same name occurs in more than one country. In these cases, the country names are added after each place name. For example:

Córdoba, *Argentina* . .
Córdoba, *Spain* . . . . .

All rivers are indexed to their mouths or confluences and are followed by the symbol →. All country names are followed by the symbol ■.

Each place name is followed by its latitude and longitude, and then its map page number and figure-letter grid reference. Both latitude and longitude are measured in degrees and minutes. There are 60 minutes in a degree. The latitude is followed by N(orth) or S(outh) and the longitude by E(ast) or W(est). The map extract on the left shows how to find a place by estimating the required distance from the nearest line of latitude or longitude on the map page. Portree is used as an example:

Portree . . . . 57°25′N 6°12′W **18** **2B**

There are 60 minutes between the lines and so to find the position of Portree an estimate has to be made. 25 parts of the 60 minutes north of the 57°N latitude line, and 12 parts of the 60 minutes west of the 6°W longitude line.

The latitude and longitude are followed by a number in bold type which refers to the number of the map page on which the place or feature appears. Portree is on page **18**.

The figure and letter which follow the page number give the grid rectangle on the map within which the place or feature appears. The grid is formed by the lines of latitude and longitude. The columns are labelled at the top and bottom of the map with a letter and the rows at the sides of the map with a number. Portree is in the grid square where row **2** crosses column **B**.

A

Aalborg . . . . 57° 2′N 9°54′ E **32** **4N**
Aarhus . . . . 56° 8′N 10°11′ E **32** **4P**
Aba . . . . 5°10′N 7°19′ E **52** **2C**
Ābādān . . . . 30°22′N 48°20′ E **48** **3E**
Abakan . . . . 53°40′N 91°10′ E **41** **4K**
ABC Islands . . . . 12°15′N 69° 0′W **63** **5L**
Abeokuta . . . . 7° 3′N 3°19′ E **52** **2B**
Aberdare . . . . 51°43′N 3°27′W **17** **5C**
Aberdare Range . . . 0°15′S 36°50′ E **53** **3B**
Aberdeen . . . . 57° 9′N 2° 5′W **18** **2F**
Abergavenny . . . . . . 51°49′N 3° 1′W **17** **5C**
Aberystwyth . . . . . . 52°25′N 4° 5′W **17** **4B**
Abidjan . . . . 5°26′N 3°58′W **51** **5B**
Abu Dhabi . . . . 24°28′N 54°22′ E **48** **5F**
Abuja . . . . 9° 5′N 7°32′ E **52** **2C**
Acapulco . . . . 16°51′N 99°55′W **62** **4D**
Accra . . . . 5°35′N 0° 6′W **52** **2A**
Accrington . . . . 53°45′N 2°22′W **16** **3D**
Achill Island . . . . 53°58′N 10° 1′W **19** **3A**
Aconcagua . . . . 32°39′S 70° 0′W **64** **7D**
Acre . . . . 9° 1′S 71° 0′W **66** **4A**
Ad Dammām . . . . . . 26°20′N 50° 5′ E **48** **4F**
Adamawa Highlands 7°20′N 12°20′ E **52** **2D**
Adana . . . . 37° 0′N 35°16′ E **35** **4L**
Adare, Cape . . . . 71° 0′S 171° 0′ E **67** **11E**
Addis Ababa . . . . . . 9° 2′N 38°42′ E **51** **5F**
Adelaide . . . . 34°52′S 138°30′ E **54** **8G**
Adelaide Island . . . . 67°15′S 68°30′W **67** **17D**
Adélie Land . . . . 68° 0′S 140° 0′ E **67** **10D**
Aden . . . . 12°45′N 45° 0′ E **46** **5C**
Aden, Gulf of . . . . . . 12°30′N 47°30′ E **46** **5C**
Adriatic Sea . . . . 43° 0′N 16° 0′ E **36** **3F**
Ægean Sea . . . . 38°30′N 25° 0′ E **35** **4J**
Aeolian Islands . . . . 38°30′N 14°57′ E **36** **5E**
Afghanistan ■ . . . . . 33° 0′N 65° 0′ E **46** **3E**
Africa . . . . 10° 0′N 20° 0′ E **50** **5E**
Agra . . . . 27°17′N 77°58′ E **46** **4F**
Aguascalientes . . . . 21°53′N 102°18′W **62** **3D**
Ahmadabad . . . . 23° 0′N 72°40′ E **46** **4F**
Ahvāz . . . . 31°20′N 48°40′ E **48** **3E**
Ailsa Craig . . . . 55°15′N 5° 6′W **18** **4C**
Aïr . . . . 18°30′N 8° 0′ E **50** **4C**
Airdrie . . . . 55°52′N 3°57′W **18** **4E**
Aire → . . . . 53°43′N 0°55′W **13** **5F**
Aix-en-Provence . . . 43°32′N 5°27′ E **33** **11L**
Ajaccio . . . . 41°55′N 8°40′ E **33** **12N**
Akita . . . . 39°45′N 140° 7′ E **45** **3D**
Akosombo Dam . . . 6°20′N 0° 5′ E **52** **2B**
Akron . . . . 41° 5′N 81°31′W **59** **2K**
Aksu . . . . 41° 5′N 80°10′ E **42** **2C**
Al ‘Ayn . . . . 24°15′N 55°45′ E **48** **5G**
Al Aziziyah . . . . 32°30′N 13° 1′ E **34** **5F**
Al Ḩillah . . . . 32°30′N 44°25′ E **48** **3D**
Al Hufūf . . . . 25°25′N 49°45′ E **48** **4E**
Al Jubayl . . . . 27° 0′N 49°50′ E **48** **4E**
Al Kūt . . . . 32°30′N 46° 0′ E **48** **3E**
Al Mubarraz . . . . 25°30′N 49°40′ E **48** **4E**
Alabama . . . . 33° 0′N 87° 0′W **59** **4J**
Alabama → . . . . 31° 8′N 87°57′W **59** **4J**
Alagoas . . . . 9° 0′S 36° 0′W **66** **4H**
Åland Islands . . . . . . 60°15′N 20° 0′ E **31** **3D**
Alaska . . . . 64° 0′N 154° 0′W **57** **3D**
Alaska, Gulf of . . . . . 58° 0′N 145° 0′W **56** **4E**
Alaska Peninsula . . . 56° 0′N 159° 0′W **56** **4D**
Alaska Range . . . . . . 62°50′N 151° 0′W **56** **3D**
Albacete . . . . 39° 0′N 1°50′W **33** **13H**
Albania ■ . . . . 41° 0′N 20° 0′ E **35** **3G**
Albany, *Australia* . . 35° 1′S 117°58′ E **54** **9C**
Albany, *U.S.A.* . . . . . 42°39′N 73°45′W **59** **2M**
Albuquerque . . . . . . 35° 5′N 106°39′W **58** **3E**
Aldabra Islands . . . . 9°22′S 46°28′ E **51** **6G**
Aldeburgh . . . . 52°10′N 1°37′ E **17** **4H**
Alderney . . . . 49°42′N 2°11′W **17** **7D**
Aleppo . . . . 36°10′N 37°15′ E **48** **2C**
Ålesund . . . . 62°28′N 6°12′ E **31** **3B**
Aleutian Islands . . . 52° 0′N 175° 0′W **68** **2A**
Alexander Island . . . 69° 0′S 70° 0′W **67** **17D**
Alexandria . . . . 31°13′N 29°58′ E **48** **3A**
Algarve . . . . 36°58′N 8°20′W **33** **14D**
Algeria ■ . . . . 28°30′N 2° 0′ E **51** **3C**
Algiers . . . . 36°42′N 3° 8′ E **51** **2C**
Alicante . . . . 38°23′N 0°30′W **33** **13H**
Alice Springs . . . . . . 23°40′S 133°50′ E **54** **6F**
Allahabad . . . . 25°25′N 81°58′ E **46** **4G**
Allegheny Mountains 38°15′N 80°10′W **59** **3L**
Allen, Bog of . . . . . . 53°15′N 7° 0′W **19** **3D**
Allen, Lough . . . . . . 54° 8′N 8° 4′W **19** **2C**
Alloa . . . . 56° 7′N 3°47′W **18** **3E**
Alma Ata . . . . 43°15′N 76°57′ E **40** **5H**
Almería . . . . 36°52′N 2°27′W **33** **14G**
Alness . . . . 57°41′N 4°16′W **18** **2D**
Alnwick . . . . 55°24′N 1°42′W **16** **1E**
Alps . . . . 46°30′N 9°30′ E **33** **9N**
Altai . . . . 46°40′N 92°45′ E **40** **4J**
Altay . . . . 47°48′N 88°10′ E **42** **2C**
Altun Shan . . . . 38°30′N 88° 0′ E **42** **3C**
Amapá . . . . 1°40′N 52° 0′W **66** **2E**
Amarillo . . . . 35°13′N 101°50′W **58** **3F**
Amazon → . . . . 0° 5′S 50° 0′W **66** **3E**
Amazonas . . . . 5° 0′S 65° 0′W **66** **4B**
Ambon . . . . 3°43′S 128°12′ E **47** **7L**
American Highland . 73° 0′S 75° 0′ E **67** **6E**
American Samoa . . 14°20′S 170° 0′W **55** **4S**
Amery Ice Shelf . . . . 69°30′S 72° 0′ E **67** **6D**
Amiens . . . . 49°54′N 2°16′ E **33** **8J**
Amlwch . . . . 53°24′N 4°20′W **16** **3B**
‘Ammān . . . . 31°57′N 35°52′ E **48** **3C**
Amritsar . . . . 31°35′N 74°57′ E **46** **3F**
Amsterdam . . . . 52°23′N 4°54′ E **32** **6L**
Amudarya → . . . . . 43°58′N 59°34′ E **40** **5F**
Amundsen Sea . . . . 72° 0′S 115° 0′W **67** **15E**
Amur → . . . . 52°56′N 141°10′ E **41** **4Q**
An Najaf . . . . 32° 3′N 44°15′ E **48** **3D**
An Nāşirīyah . . . . . . 31° 0′N 46°15′ E **48** **3E**
Anápolis . . . . 16°15′S 48°50′W **66** **6F**
Anatolia . . . . 39° 0′N 30° 0′ E **48** **2B**
Anchorage . . . . 61°13′N 149°54′W **57** **3E**
Ancona . . . . 43°38′N 13°30′ E **36** **3D**
Andalucía . . . . 37°35′N 5° 0′W **33** **14F**
Andaman Islands . . 12°30′N 92°45′ E **46** **5H**
Andaman Sea . . . . . 13° 0′N 96° 0′ E **38** **7L**
Andes . . . . 10° 0′S 75°53′W **64** **5D**
Andizhan . . . . 41°10′N 72°15′ E **42** **2B**
Andorra ■ . . . . 42°30′N 1°30′ E **33** **11J**
Andover . . . . 51°12′N 1°29′W **17** **5E**
Aneto, Pico de . . . . . 42°37′N 0°40′ E **33** **11J**
Angara → . . . . 58° 5′N 94°20′ E **41** **4K**
Angel Falls . . . . 5°57′N 62°30′W **63** **6M**
Angers . . . . 47°30′N 0°35′W **33** **9H**
Anglesey . . . . 53°17′N 4°20′W **16** **3B**
Angola ■ . . . . 12° 0′S 18° 0′ E **51** **7D**
Angoulême . . . . 45°39′N 0°10′ E **33** **10J**
Angus . . . . 56°46′N 2°56′W **15** **3E**
Ankara . . . . 39°57′N 32°54′ E **35** **4K**
Annaba . . . . 36°50′N 7°46′ E **34** **4E**
Annan . . . . 54°59′N 3°16′W **18** **5E**
Annan → . . . . 54°58′N 3°16′W **18** **4E**
Annapolis . . . . 38°59′N 76°30′W **59** **3L**
Annobón . . . . 1°25′S 5°36′ E **50** **6C**
Anshan . . . . 41° 5′N 122°58′ E **43** **2G**
Antalya . . . . 36°52′N 30°45′ E **35** **4K**
Antananarivo . . . . . . 18°55′S 47°31′ E **51** **7G**
Antarctic Peninsula . 67° 0′S 60° 0′W **67** **18D**
Antarctica . . . . 90° 0′S 0° 0′W **67** **3F**
Antigua & Barbuda ■ 17°20′N 61°48′W **63** **4M**
Antofagasta . . . . 23°50′S 70°30′W **65** **6D**
Antrim . . . . 54°43′N 6°14′W **19** **2E**
Antrim, Mountains of 55° 3′N 6°14′W **19** **2E**
Antrim & Newtownabbey . . 54°40′N 6°11′W **15** **4C**
Antwerp . . . . 51°13′N 4°25′ E **32** **7L**
Anvers Island . . . . . 64°30′S 63°40′W **67** **17D**
Aomori . . . . 40°45′N 140°45′ E **45** **2D**
Aoraki Mount Cook . 43°36′S 170° 9′ E **55** **10P**
Apennines . . . . 44°30′N 10° 0′ E **36** **3D**
Apia . . . . 13°50′S 171°50′W **55** **4S**
Appalachian Mountains . . . . . . 38° 0′N 80° 0′W **59** **3K**
Appleby-in-Westmorland . . . . 54°35′N 2°29′W **16** **2D**
Aqaba . . . . 29°31′N 35° 0′ E **48** **4C**
Arabia . . . . 25° 0′N 45° 0′ E **38** **6F**
Arabian Sea . . . . 16° 0′N 65° 0′ E **46** **5E**
Aracaju . . . . 10°55′S 37° 4′W **66** **5H**
Araçatuba . . . . 21°10′S 50°30′W **66** **7E**
Araguaia → . . . . 5°21′S 48°41′W **66** **4F**
Arāk . . . . 34° 0′N 49°40′ E **48** **3E**
Araks → . . . . 40° 5′N 48°29′ E **48** **1E**
Aral Sea . . . . 45° 0′N 58°20′ E **40** **5F**
Aran Islands . . . . . . 53° 6′N 9°38′W **19** **3B**
Ararat, Mount . . . . . 39°50′N 44°15′ E **48** **2D**
Arbroath . . . . 56°34′N 2°35′W **18** **3F**
Arctic Ocean . . . . . . 78° 0′N 160° 0′W **67** **18B**
Ardabīl . . . . 38°15′N 48°18′ E **48** **2E**
Ardnamurchan, Point of . . . . 56°43′N 6°14′W **18** **3B**
Ardrossan . . . . 55°39′N 4°49′W **18** **4D**
Ards & North Down 54°32′N 5°39′W **15** **4D**
Ards Peninsula . . . . 54°33′N 5°34′W **19** **2F**
Arequipa . . . . 16°20′S 71°30′W **65** **5D**
Argentina ■ . . . . 35° 0′S 66° 0′W **65** **7E**
Argun → . . . . 53°20′N 121°28′ E **43** **1F**
Argyle, Lake . . . . 16°20′S 128°40′ E **54** **5E**
Argyll . . . . 56°10′N 5°20′W **18** **3C**
Argyll & Bute . . . . . . 56°13′N 5°28′W **15** **3D**
Arica . . . . 18°32′S 70°20′W **65** **5D**
Aripuanã → . . . . 5° 7′S 60°25′W **66** **4C**
Arizona . . . . 34° 0′N 112° 0′W **58** **4D**
Arkaig, Loch . . . . . . 56°59′N 5°10′W **18** **3C**
Arkansas . . . . 35° 0′N 92°30′W **59** **4H**
Arkansas → . . . . 33°47′N 91° 4′W **59** **4H**
Arkhangelsk . . . . 64°38′N 40°36′ E **31** **3J**
Arklow . . . . 52°48′N 6°10′W **19** **4E**
Armagh . . . . 54°21′N 6°39′W **19** **2E**
Armagh, Bansbridge & Craigavon . . . . . 54°20′N 6°28′W **15** **4C**
Armenia ■ . . . . 40°20′N 45° 0′ E **48** **1D**
Arnhem . . . . 51°58′N 5°55′ E **32** **7L**
Arnhem Land . . . . . 13°10′S 134°30′ E **54** **4F**
Arran . . . . 55°34′N 5°12′W **18** **4C**
Arranmore . . . . 55° 0′N 8°30′W **19** **1C**
Aru Islands . . . . 6° 0′S 134°30′ E **47** **7M**
Aruba . . . . 12°30′N 70° 0′W **63** **5L**
Arusha . . . . 3°20′S 36°40′ E **53** **3B**
Arvayheer . . . . 46°15′N 102°48′ E **42** **2E**
As Sulaymānīyah, *Iraq* . . . . 35°35′N 45°29′ E **48** **2E**
As Sulaymānīyah, *Saudi Arabia* . . . . 24° 9′N 47°18′ E **48** **5E**
Asahikawa . . . . 43°46′N 142°22′ E **45** **2D**
Asamankese . . . . . . 5°50′N 0°40′W **52** **2A**
Ascension Island . . . 7°57′S 14°23′W **51** **6A**
Ashford . . . . 51° 8′N 0°53′ E **17** **5G**
Ashington . . . . 55°11′N 1°33′W **16** **1E**
Ashkhabad . . . . 37°58′N 58°24′ E **48** **2G**
Ashton under Lyne . 53°29′N 2° 6′W **16** **3D**
Asmara . . . . 15°19′N 38°55′ E **51** **4F**
Assam . . . . 26° 0′N 93° 0′ E **46** **4H**
Astana . . . . 51°10′N 71°30′ E **40** **4H**
Astrakhan . . . . 46°25′N 48° 5′ E **38** **5E**
Asunción . . . . 25°10′S 57°30′W **65** **6F**
Aswân . . . . 24° 4′N 32°57′ E **48** **5B**
Asyût . . . . 27°11′N 31° 4′ E **48** **4B**
Aţ Tā’if . . . . 21° 5′N 40°27′ E **48** **5D**
Atacama Desert . . . . 24° 0′S 69°20′W **64** **6E**
Athens . . . . 37°58′N 23°43′ E **35** **4H**
Athlone . . . . 53°25′N 7°56′W **19** **3D**
Athy . . . . 53° 0′N 7° 0′W **19** **4E**
Atlanta . . . . 33°45′N 84°23′W **59** **4K**
Atlantic Ocean . . . . . 0° 0′ 20° 0′W **68** **3G**
Atlas Mountains . . . 32°30′N 5° 0′W **50** **2B**
Auckland . . . . 36°52′S 174°46′ E **55** **9P**
Augsburg . . . . 48°25′N 10°52′ E **33** **8P**
Augusta . . . . 44°19′N 69°47′W **59** **2N**
Austin . . . . 30°17′N 97°45′W **58** **4G**
Australia ■ . . . . 23° 0′S 135° 0′ E **54** **6D**
Australian Capital Territory (A.C.T.) . 35°30′S 149° 0′ E **54** **9J**
Austria ■ . . . . 47° 0′N 14° 0′ E **34** **2F**
Aviemore . . . . 57°12′N 3°50′W **18** **2E**
Avignon . . . . 43°57′N 4°50′ E **33** **11L**
Avon →, *Bristol* . . . 51°29′N 2°41′W **17** **5D**
Avon →, *Dorset* . . . 50°44′N 1°46′W **17** **6E**
Avon →, *Warwickshire* . . . . 52° 0′N 2° 8′W **17** **4D**